Voice Building
for
Choirs

Wilhelm Ehmann
Frauke Haasemann

English Translation by Brenda Smith

ISBN Number: 0-937276-02-2

Library of Congress Catalog Card Number: 82-081988

Original Edition: Wilhelm Ehmann / Frauke Haasemann
Chorische Stimmbildung. Hilfen zu stimmlicher Forderung.
Revised Edition 1981
Copyright ©1981 by Bärenreiter-Verlag Kassel
This Edition licensed by Bärenreiter-Verlag Kassel - Basel - London
to Hinshaw Music, Inc. 1982
P.O. Box 470, Chapel Hill, NC 27514

Table of Contents

Preface To Chapter A

Voice training in an amateur choir is of special importance. Some voice teachers would oppose attempting to improve an individual voice in a choral rehearsal. I can understand this attitude if one interprets the mission of choral voice training as a means of cultivating the solo voice. It has been my experience in hundreds of choral workshops and weekly choral rehearsals that effective and efficient voice building can exercise challenge and advance a choir immeasurably. In some cases, the musical work cannot be mastered without choral voice training, and a balanced sound cannot be achieved. Just as it is obvious that an instrumentalist must learn an instrument (no one could play a Bach fugue without having the necessary instruction), so the vocal mechanism must be studied and guided if it is to be used for an artistic purpose.

The voice belongs to two realms simultaneously. It participates in our lives at the artistic and at the functional levels. It is used for speaking, shouting, crying as well as for singing. This has its advantages and its disadvantages, for as one use may benefit another, so may it handicap another. If one handles his voice and body properly, and if the body is conditioned and relaxed, with good breathing and posture, the process of singing will be helped. Further, good voice lessons can teach the student important information about various aspects of life and enhance his self-confidence. The procedures vary but no matter where one begins, the artistic and physical elements of singing will meet again and again.

One may say that the process of singing is basically the same for the professional and amateur: a voice box is a voice box. But the ways of bringing a voice to its best work are diverse. For one student, the teacher needs to be more pedagogical; for another, more technical; for another, more philosophical. One student learns more quickly when the instruction provides clear details of the vocal mechanism, while another student is inhibited by this knowledge.

In any case, the fundamental principle is that one should strive for the "natural." That is, the natural functions of the voice must serve the artistic needs for good singing. From this perspective, choral voice training leads into the science of singing.

With both professionals and amateurs, the pedagogue should rely on exercises related to daily life, designed to meet the needs of each student, singer or group. A method must be chosen that the singer can apply easily to choral singing, because the conductor cannot observe the habits of each singer. The exercises given here will help to demonstrate such a method, using normal activities from daily life.

Of course, one should be conscious of the dangers associated with the misuse of such an approach. Exercises based on children's games and habitual daily activities are of no use if presented in a haphazard way; discipline must be maintained. Thus choral voice building sessions must be carefully planned. Every good voice teacher realizes the importance of timed, sensible vocalises and although these exercises can be used to develop any voice, amateur or professional, it is to be understood that a foundation of sound individual vocal technique is invaluable. It is important for me to emphasize that this booklet is not intended as a manual for choral voice training or as a progressive study for the cultivation of the human voice. Nature has supplied us with many functions which can be lifted out of their original settings and applied systematically elsewhere, and the same principle applies to the improvement of singing by stressing the natural functioning of the vocal mechanism. The exercises outline only the beginning of the course for development, and are not to be considered as a comprehensive method for voice building.

Nature gives us an effective vocal mechanism: the infant breathes and speaks in a healthy way. During the process of human development, through the shocks of puberty, the strains of communal life, the lack of physical activity, the impurities of the environment and the like, most voices are impaired. Restoring the natural production through sound choral voice training poses certain special problems for the amateur singer. For example, the amateur's approach to singing is much different from that of the professional singer, and he or she will often not respond well to a method of instruction which incorporates technical terms. Terminology about vocal technique is apt to be incomprehensible to the singer. The voice of the amateur is a natural part of the body; music is a product of life and there is a freshness about this outlook which one should not destroy. The amateur will object to any means of vocal training which is considered artificial as an imposition upon a personal freedom and he or she will expect the voice to be developed as naturally as it was conceived. The more amateur the choir, the more difficult it may be to introduce voice training exercises. It will take a bit of cunning and imagination to bring the singer to develop a singing ability without making the process obvious, and it will not be enough to sing examples, nor to beat the singers over the head with exercises or to explain their technical implications. In fact, one must often avoid being too specific about vocal technique, thereby allowing for the power of the singer's creative imagination.

The challenge then is to improve tone production, artistic sensibilities and musical understanding without losing spontaneity, to release the choir from pedantic note learning and free it for singing. The dull rehearsal must be transformed into an exciting musical event. The teaching of a new piece must happen in an atmosphere of real music-making: it is work and play all in one.

WILHELM EHMANN

Chapter A of this book appeared as a separate text under the title *Chorische Stimmbildung,* Bärenreiter (1958, third German printing, 1979).

Foreword To The Expanded Edition, Chapters B and C

For many centuries the choral art of Europe was developed by professional musicians. The French Revolution with its outcry for freedom, equality and brotherhood influenced the Swiss choral conductor Hans Georg Naegeli (1773-1836) and the German music director Karl Friedrich Zelter (1758-1832). These men sought to bring choral singing from the 'aristocratic' to the 'democratic' level so that the people themselves could participate. Many generations shared their enthusiasm. Choral activities moved from the narrow scope of the select professional ensemble to the broad base of the amateur choral group. Naegeli recognized the necessity for teaching the fundamentals of singing as they apply to choral music in order to establish a deeper sense of fraternity. Choral singing became an organ of society. Naegeli collected his principles in the book *Gesangbildungslehre nach Grundsaetzen Pestalozzis* (1809) translated *Voice Training Textbook based on the Fundamentals presented by Pestalozzi*. This handbook was intended for public schools and for the community at large. Up until this time, professional choirs had gleaned their personnel from the ranks of the privately educated.

Today we find ourselves in much the same circumstance: amateur choirs perform large choral masterpieces. Because the musical training in public schools varies in its content and intensity, it behooves the choral conductor to seek methods of completing the amateur singer's choral education. It is at this point that choral voice building becomes an attractive alternative.

As any student of singing is aware, there are many methods of vocal technique, each dictating what is "right" and "wrong." In various cultures and on several levels of musical ability and understanding, the voice may be treated differently. That which is considered "right" for one situation is recognized as being "wrong" for another: for example, the definitions and usages of Bel Canto, Heldentenor, Folklore, Popular music, Jazz. The exercises contained in this book deal with the realm of Bel Canto technique. It is clear that the principles of the Bel Canto tradition have been applied to the development of a 'sound ideal' through contrasting epochs of musical composition (see C, b-f). We will present technical helps designed to achieve the results of these principles for particular sound ideals.

As stated in the foreword to the first edition, musical exercises can be derived from daily activities and can guide the choral singer to an artistic use of the voice. Chapters B and C of this book expand upon possibilities previously mentioned. Frauke Haasemann has conducted numerous workshops for amateur and professional choral conductors of church choirs, boy choirs, large civic organization as well as professional choirs and opera choruses throughout Europe and the United States. The method described below has proven itself applicable to all types of choral involvement. The individual exercises should be selected to accommodate the age, musicality, training and mentality of the singers. Note that the subject matter of Chapter A corresponds directly to the examples given in Chapters B and C.

Choral voice building is an emergency system: one cannot expect to create a group of solo singers through these added technical skills. It is not possible to improve major individual vocal problems (tremolo, difficulties caused by nodules on the vocal cords, etc.) by group vocal techniques. Private voice instruction should be suggested for the correction of such deficiencies.

Choral voice building is a means of:

1. Awakening the choral singer's interest and involvement
2. Instilling a sense of need for vocal growth
3. Helping the singer recognize his or her own vocal potential.

Choral voice building is a necessity:

The choral conductor can accomplish the musical and artistic goals with a choir which would have been technically unattainable without the use of choral voice building.

Many of the exercises which are given below are useful to the singer only when performed in a group (for example, the question and answer games, the echo games, butter-churning).

Most functions in choral singing are based upon exaggeration; that is, the subtleties which a solo singer would employ must be multiplied by the entire group. The converse being true: an error is amplified in an ensemble. For example, the degree of choral articulation is double that required for the articulation of solo works.

Choral singers must consider themselves an integral part of the whole and engage in the learning process accordingly. They should proceed in growth with an acute awareness of their neighbor's progress from breathing and phonating to phrasing and dynamic control. We speak of choral "bodies" whose "members" are the singers and the conductor inclusive. Choral voice building can provide such a framework.

A choral sound does not represent the sum of the individual voices, but is rather the addition of an unknown quantity to the voices. This indescribable element supplies the "choral" quality to sound—the sense of ensemble. Therefore, the trained singer must reduce the vocal force if one wishes to sing in a choir. Choral voice building can aid the singer in determining a role in the development of the sound.

The perceptive choral conductor imagines distinctive sounds and styles of singing for each epoch of music history. These sounds and styles can be created with choral resources (see C, I, II).

Because of the nature of the subject, it is difficult to formulate sentences to describe the procedures for choral voice building. Perhaps it seems contradictory that one cannot write succinctly about music; however, music is transmitted best as music. Furthermore, the end results of the vocal exercises prescribed below are neither visible nor tangible. We must quicken our imaginations to create new sounds. The ear will determine the quality of the result. Thus the choral conductor should attempt to test each of the exercises with his or her own voice. A demonstration of the exercise will be of more immediate assistance to singers than any written or spoken explanation.

A choral conductor who feels incapable of presenting choral voice building exercises to a choir may wish to call upon a professional voice teacher or a trained choir member to fulfill the assignment. In any case, one must resist the temptation to employ the organ or the piano as a mechanism for voice building because of the percussive nature of both instruments. The conductor who is involved with performing as an accompanist for the choir is not capable of hearing critically.

WILHELM EHMANN, FRAUKE HAASEMANN
Herford, Princeton, 1980

Acknowledgements:

We wish to thank Dr. and Mrs. David Willis and Dr. Joseph Flummerfelt for their assistance in the production of this text.

FRAUKE HAASEMANN/BRENDA SMITH

Translator's Note

The nature of choral music itself denotes a collection of peoples, skills and cultural orientation. The text which follows is intended to assist the work of choral conductors, vocal teachers, solo singers and the students of all three. It would be impossible to address these various factions without defining a brief glossary of terms. The vocabulary of the artist in any field is quite specific to a concept. In the area of vocal study, there is a wide range of associations between sensations and results which carry several connotations.

To avoid debating the effective use of any particular phrase or name, let us state clearly the language applicable to this text. Vocal jargon relates to three aspects: imagery, anatomy and phonetics.

Imagery is depicted in the body of this text by both authors as a basic resource. In all cases, an example is given circumscribing a common function or activity (for example, the utterance of a farm animal or the roar of a passing vehicle).

The anatomy of the vocal mechanism has complicated headings for

xi

medical use. Many structural and moveable parts of the body are of special interest to the singer. It is important that the conductor and teacher strive to understand thoroughly the mechanics of the singer's anatomy. Singers themselves must be acquainted with general functions of the vocal mechanism. It may suffice to say that the singer must recognize the location and function of the various parts of the body, in order to note any dysfunctions independently. A series of general terms are defined in the glossary for this purpose.

The International Phonetic Alphabet is a common bond between singers and linguists. It is adapted to the German and English references in the examples given here to insure that the transliteration of syllables will be interpreted properly. An abbreviated directory to the IPA follows:

VOWELS

IPA Symbol	Example
[a]	target
[ae]	mat
[e]	may
[ɛ]	met
[i]	me
[ɪ]	mit
[o]	moment
[ɔ]	paw
[u]	moon
[ʊ]	foot
[ʌ]	flung
[ə]	tablet
[ɜ]	remember

MIXED VOWELS

IPA Symbol	Example
[ɛ]	Tränen
[ɣ]	Tübingen
[y]	küssen
[ø]	Lösung
[œ]	möchte

DIPHTHONGS

IPA Symbol	Example
[eɪ]	may
[oʊ]	so
[aʊ]	bow
[aɪ]	tie
[ɔɪ]	rejoice

DIPHTHONGS AND TRIPHTHONGS

IPA Symbol	Example
[əə]	mar
[eə]	chair
[iə]	tear
[ʊə]	demure
[aɪə]	tire
[aʊə]	bower

CONSONANTS

IPA Symbol	Example
[p]	pop
[b]	baby
[t]	top
[d]	do
[k]	keep
[g]	gang
[m]	mother
[n]	nine
[ŋ]	singing
[f]	four
[v]	vigor
[s]	sister
[z]	zooms
[θ]	thither
[ð]	the
[ʃ]	shoes
[ʒ]	fusion
[tʃ]	charm

xiii

[dʒ]	justice	
[h]	here	
[w]	woman	
[hw]	whither	
[j]	young	
[l]	little	
[r]	right	
[ç]	mich ⎤	GERMAN
[x]	mach ⎦	only

The text is organized as a handbook for its readers. There are numerous cross-references to assist in providing explanations for uncommon expressions or for further study. The most creative use of the suggestions given below will achieve a diversity of direction to the choral/vocal difficulties presented in the repertoire of any amateur or professional group. It is important to view the text as a guidebook to an imaginative pedagogical technique.

BRENDA SMITH
Princeton, 1980

Voice Building
for
Choirs

Chapter A

THE USE OF DAILY ACTIVITIES FOR CHORAL VOICE BUILDING EXERCISES

I. POSTURE

a. Gymnastic exercises and games

Gymnastics and game sports should be encouraged, because they produce the flexibility and relaxation needed for singing. Body awareness is heightened, preparing the way for body-mind coordination. Physical activities open the resonating cavities of the body while strengthening the muscles essential for breathing (i.e., diaphragm, abdominal muscles, etc.). Suggested forms of exercise are: movement games, ball games, swimming, jogging, hopping and stretching exercises.

Sample Exercises:

1. Lay down and press the back to the floor. The body stretches and relaxes automatically.
2. Pair off the singers in groups of two. The couples stand back to back, pressing at various points up and down the back.
3. Churning butter, crawling on all fours, rocking back and forth in a chair, playing leap frog, playing 'dead.'

Such games should never be strenuous, rather relaxing.

b. General relaxation and posture exercises

Relaxation and posture exercises should be related directly to the singing process in actuality or in imagination: for example, waving 'hello' and 'good-bye,' throwing stones or balls, shaking the head with various degrees of intensity, ringing bells, pretending that the body is a bell being rung from the spine (the body's vertical axis), or from the waist (the horizontal axis), swaying, carrying a weight on the head, picking fruit and stretching as much as possible, boxing, hitting stones together, balancing on a curb or balcony railing, stepping over an imaginary line.

Music-making requires a loose, flexible body feeling. With the eyes closed, imagine the body as a tolling bell hung from the top of the head. Play a game of chase. Imitate a plane by stretching out the arms to either side. Raise the heels from the floor and lower them. Collapse and straighten the body repeatedly.

c. Application of physical exercise to singing

The following activities can take place while singing and serve to relax the body inwardly and outwardly. When singing canons with "ding-dong" refrains such as *Are You Sleeping?*, encourage the singer to imitate the bell ringer. While singing a sailor song or sea chanty, shake imaginary beads of water from the body. Wave 'farewell' with the hand after a sad melody. Snap, clap or step to the rhythm of any familiar song.

These exercises should be full of active imagination in order to achieve good coordination of the body-mind processes.

Finally, remember to build posture from the foundation: that is, stand firmly on both feet, the heels apart. Concentrate on the bottoms of the feet. Try to feel the floor. The knees are flexed; the hips are free, the shoulders high. The head seems to extend from the neck with plenty of room to move in any direction. The head rests on the spine. The throat should not be bent nor should the face be wrinkled—except 'perhaps' in a smile. Each singer stands so that he can see the conductor without straining (see Ehmann, *Choral Directing*, Section A, pp. 1 ff.).

II. BREATHING

Breathing should be a passive function. The breathing musculature is not an 'air pump' for singing. One must learn to wait for the breath to come by itself. Allow the choir members to stand quietly. Begin with exhalation through the mouth. Then hold the breath for a brief interval and listen for the heartbeat until the air flows in through the nose without effort. The length of time for suspending the air should be increased gradually. Count the number of heartbeats or whisper a sentence to the choir.

Certain sports can aid diaphragmatic action, such as: jogging, hopping, romping, tossing a ball or any game which requires continuous bending or reaching.

Other activities incorporate the swinging of the hip region with the diaphragm as the center: lawn mowing, sawing, thrashing, sickling, wood chopping. When stacking a pile of bricks, collecting fruit or gathering mushrooms, the same stepping and bending motion is necessary. Use these imaginary games to prepare singers for breathing exercises.

Proper breathing should be developed as a conscious habit. When possible, inhalation should occur through the nose. It is an involuntary function. Exhalation should happen through the mouth and may be voluntary. The nose learns the sensation of incoming air, moving in a rhythmic manner. No sound should accompany inhalation. While singing, one inhales through the nose with the mouth slightly opened to obtain the maximum amount of air as quickly as possible.

Sample Exercises:

1. Try elevating the arms above the head during inhalation and then lowering them for exhalation.

2. Rest a hand on the abdominal wall and at the small of the back to test the reaction of the muscles to diaphragmatic movement. These regions combine to form the so-called 'breath ring.'
3. Yawning, sighing, laughing are among the images which encourage deep breathing.
4. Smell the overwhelming scent of a freshly cut rose.
5. Taste a luscious ripe peach.
   Relaxation and thorough use of the breathing apparatus are inherent in these activities.

Breathing exercises can be inserted into the choir rehearsal. For instance, reach for a flower or a piece of fruit when singing a song about Spring or Fall. Wandering and hunting songs provide similar possibilities. Breathe the fresh, scented air of the outdoors. When singing a sad song, sigh heavily. A laughing song can strengthen the diaphragm, too (see Ehmann, *Choral Directing*, pp. 6 ff, 15 ff for further explanation regarding breathing exercises for the rehearsal plan).

Because breathing is the basis for good singing, concentrated breath exercises are essential.

a. Ways to build diaphragmatic control through relaxation and proper air compression

1. *Hunting game:* Call "piff, puff, poof!" The consonants *p* and *f* compress and expel the air. A reflex action occurs in the diaphragm. There is a rippling motion in the abdominal wall. Practice 'shooting' from a reclining position, so that each singer can feel the motion of the abdominal wall against the floor, created by the diaphragm. Then hold the revolver at hip level, resting one hand on the small of the back. With each shot, the hand will check the action of the breathing muscles.
The sounds "piff, puff, poof" can be sung to different pitches, in scale passages or as melodic fragments.

2. *Machine gun game:* Call "tack, tack, tack" . . . While the consonant *t* exercises the tip of the tongue and the front portion of the hard palate, the consonant *k* causes compression between the back of the tongue and the rear portion of the hard palate. Allow the machine gun to be shot at various calibers, slower and faster in repetition and then at different pitch levels.

3. *Horse game:* A horse snorts "prh" . . . The sensation of the rolled *r* will bring the lips forward in a relaxed fashion. This activity develops a feeling for air compression and expulsion while creating flexibility in the face and throat muscles.

4. *Sighing, whimpering, hiccuping:* A constriction occurs between the back of the tongue and the back of the hard palate. The vocal cords should not be approximated completely if possible; but rather, a muted and undetermined sound should be uttered. Note the air compression and its reaction in the abdominal wall, back and hips. Encourage the activity to happen naturally. It is a release to burp or to groan. When groaning, the

air compression occurs as the lungs expel the deoxygenated air. When sobbing and hiccuping, air is brought into the body. The concept of air 'falling' into the body is a significant one. This exercise will be used again for developing more space in the pharyngeal region and for quick catch breaths.

5. *Train game:* The lungs are filled with air like a steam engine. The locomotive begins to move and the steam is puffed out with [tʃ], [z], [ts], or [ˈpf]. The locomotive travels slowly at first and then gains speed. The elbows can be used to simulate the movement of the piston rods. Observe the muscular action in the stomach and hip regions. The locomotive moves at full tilt with gasps at regular intervals, which can be varied. The exercise becomes a means of increasing rhythmic skill. Present patterns in 2/4, 3/4, or 4/4 with shifting accents.

b. Exercises to create a steady expulsion and use of air

Every singer must learn that the first task is breath management. A complete emptying of the air column is necessary before fresher air can be inhaled. Any muscular manipulation of the air during inhalation can be harmful.

1. *Puffing on a window:* The palms of the hand serve as an imaginary window which has frozen. Breathe against the window with an open mouth to melt the ice. With great energy, the window will be defrosted from both sides. This exercise expands the breathing mechanism and empties the lungs.

2. *Cooling the soup:* The soup is too hot to eat. Pretend that the hands form the soup bowl. Blow lightly over the soup to spread the steam. The mouth is slightly puckered. Guide the breath around the bowl and cool off all the soup.

3. *Cooling an injury:* A wound on an arm hurts. Blow the injured area with a soothing stream of air expelled through puckered lips. Direct the air toward the wound in a circular motion.

4. *Puffing at dandelions:* Each singer holds an imaginary flower in a hand and tries to blow the seeds away with as little air pressure as possible. Puff at many flowers, one after another as if romping through a field of wild flowers. Compete with one another.

5. *Playing with downfeathers:* Imagine downfeathers in the air and puff them away from below. The feathers continue to fall down. In order to force them upwards puff long blasts of air. The torso should remain under the floating feathers. The latter exercises encourage the flow of breath from the body. In a similar way, one can use the example of a celluloid ball which sweeps over a spiral or a column. Here, a controlled volume of air is needed to keep the ball balanced. Improper air pressure will send the ball sailing away.

6. *Pumping up a bicycle tire:* Imagine a bicycle inner tube. The air pours out steadily on [s] or [f] or [ʃ] through a tiny opening. Steady expendi-

ture of the air is an important consideration. When the tube is empty, it collapses. Push out the last air with both fists. Connect the tube to an electric air pump and open the vent. The air flows in very slowly. The exercise is repeated. The tube represents the lungs and the vent is the nose.

7. *Imitating a locomotive:* The locomotive expels steam on [s], [f], [ʃ].

8. *Imitating insects:* Buzz a soft, high-pitched [s] or [z], like mosquitoes. Imitate bees with a steady, low-pitched [s] or [z]. (It is important to use the voice in combination with breathing as much as possible). To create an intense column of sound, allow the forefinger to follow the movement of the mosquitoes or bees in the air. Move in rising and falling circles.

c. Exercises for restraining the air and achieving body area for proper breath support

Steady breath support will serve as the fundamental guide for tone production.

1. *Eavesdropping in the dark:* Begin by breathing out, close the eyes and listen breathlessly in the darkness. Perhaps it will help to imagine a woods. Hear the beating of the heart. The heart rate increases with anticipation. The conductor can whisper a sentence or count aloud, accumulating more syllables or numerals. Open the nose to allow air to flow in. This process encourages passive breathing, while the singer becomes attentive for other exercises which follow. (Exhalation involves the same procedure in reverse. Release the air slowly and regularly through the mouth).

2. *Diving:* Where possible, practice holding the breath when diving into the water. Do not take too much air at one time. Hold the air equivalent to the distance to be traveled. The movement of the body in the water and the air increases the feeling for body-mind coordination. Swimming helps deep breathing and is supported through arm movements.

3. *Fright:* Open the mouth suddenly and let the air fall into the body with a quick gasp "ah!" [a] The diaphragm reacts automatically. Let the breath stand still for a moment. Imagine that fear has "taken the breath away." The diaphragmatic and abdominal muscles hold the breath firmly. Relax by stretching and breathing out (This exercise could create tension if improperly used).

4. *Surprise and astonishment:* Similar to the exercise above, suggest a surprising or astonishing idea to the group. The reaction will be spontaneous (This exercise is more positive and less dangerous than the above).

5. *Diving while expelling the air:* Expel the air again and again. Try to breathe at regular intervals, exhaling approximately the same amount of air each time.

6. *Locomotive game:* By opening and closing the valves, the engine releases regular amounts of steam in recurring pulsations of [s], [ʃ] or [f]. The conductor indicates the opening and closing of the valve with hand motions. The exercise can be expanded at will.

7. *Blowing up a football:* Imagine a football which is being inflated. Hold

a finger over the hole and let the air escape in measured amounts. The singer could make any motion which seems appropriate, indicating the inflation of the ball.

8. *Silencing someone:* There is a murmuring in the crowd. Quiet the group and catch their attention by calling "psst." The column of air should be broken up at various lengths. Whisper at varying degrees of intensity. Hold a finger to the lips.

9. *Stuttering with explosive syllables:* Each new syllable produces a new explosion with [g], [k], [p], or [b]. These consonants cause compression between the tongue and the different parts of the hard palate or between the lips, respectively. The syllables should be decided upon at random, using the whole spectrum of vowel sounds. Think of short words which have the same vowel-consonant combinations.

III. VOICE BUILDING

a. Exercises to relax the body, loosen and strengthen the diaphragm and intensify breath control and tone quality

1. *Laughter:*

aa. The singer sits comfortably on a chair with feet flat on the floor. Lean against the back of the chair, straight enough for the abdominal region to be free. Ask a question which cannot be answered. The singer replies with a sarcastic "huh?" The syllable should be uttered almost involuntarily, as the head turns inquisitively. If the arms rest across the abdomen, one can feel the reaction of the diaphragm to this utterance. These laughing syllables can be repeated at desired intervals with no definite pitch levels designated.

bb. The same response happens with an expression of exclamation such as "aha!" Use these two exercises interchangably.

Expand upon these exercises by setting up specific rhythmic patterns in simple time signatures. Vary the patterns. Imagine traveling in a railroad train compartment. The train is moving at a steady, measured pace. Imitate the humming sound of the train. Note how the resonating cavities open. The tone will increase and decrease in intensity with diaphragmatic control.

cc. Use different types of laughing sounds in the same way: for instance, "hey!" or "hurray!" or a full-throated laugh of "ha!" or "ho!" Laughing lightens the spirit while activating the whole body.

dd. Change the type of laughter: for example, ringing laughter (ha!), general frivolity (hey!), hysterical laughter (yah-ha!), giggling (he-he!), repressed laughter (hoo!), jolly laughter (ho!).

ee. Suggest different types of people, who might laugh in different ways: such as, a fat man, a silly girl, a sarcastic fellow, an angry lumberjack, a playful child. Use various forms of humor which induce different responses. There are conductors who have a number of jokes for this purpose. A good sense of humor creates a pleasant atmosphere for corporate work.

ff. Assign pitches to the laughing syllables. Begin in the middle register of the voice, advancing by half step downwards and upwards.

gg. Increase the complexity of the rhythmic patterns also by juxtaposing long and short syllables.

hh. When changing the vowels, move from darker sounds to lighter ones. (Example: hoo - ho - ha - he, etc.). The darker vowels ([u], [ʊ], [o], [ɔ]) produce a lowered position for the vocal mechanism. Because the mechanism is more relaxed in this position, the sound is most likely to be well-placed. This position is the basis for all other vowel sounds. The conductor should be alert to the stability of the last sound. Do not allow the singer to relax the support but to continue a clear and steady sound to the end of the exercise. The dynamic level should not exceed mezzo-forte.

2. *Other technical staccato exercises can be developed from this example:*

Try to adjust the vowel sounds in the upper registers to create a consistency with the sounds produced in the middle register. Build the initial intervallic patterns within the range of an arpeggio.

3. Melodies:

aa. *Children's songs:* Sing familiar melodies from children's songs with laughing syllables. Be sure that all the singers agree on the intervals and sing them in tune. *London Bridge Is Falling Down, Mary Had a Little Lamb, Baa, Baa, Black Sheep* would be good songs for this purpose.

bb. *Transfer the results of these laughing exercises to the texts of these songs.* In order to prepare for part-singing, add a canon to the repertoire. Sing *Hi-ho, Anybody Home?* using the same sequence of syllables and text. Divide the group into two parts and then into more segments.

4. The technique known as *martellato* (literally 'hammering,' explained in detail in B, II, e) can be taught with these laughing syllables. Repeat a

series of laughing syllables. Group the syllables by two, three and four. Give a slight rhythmic accent to the first syllable of each group. Eliminate the consonants progressively until the entire exercise is sung on vowels with the diaphragmatic activity of laughing. Avoid the use of the aspirate *h* when singing.

b. Procedures for developing resonance and a range of overtones while improving tonal placement and consistency of registers

General relaxation is the first step to any technical approach.

1. *Yawning:* Make yawning a conscious act. The chest, throat, pharynx and mouth regions are spread. Yawn as quietly as possible. Yawn again with a groan of satisfaction. Be sure that the jaw and the throat are free.

2. *Falling to sleep:* Sitting in a train compartment or in an arm chair, rest the head in the corner or to one side. The body remains relaxed. The jaw falls by itself and the tongue lies passively in the mouth. Snore peacefully.

3. *Nutcracker game:* Pretend to be a nutcracker with a soldier's form. A handle operates the jaw. Place a nut in the cracker's mouth and crack it; release the jaw.

4. *Shaking the head:* Shake the head emphatically as if in negation. Allow the jaw and the tongue to fall loosely. Avoid any sort of tension.

5. *Bleating sheep:* Make a bleating sound (bl [ɛ]) a number of times. Nod the head with eyes closed and drop the jaw. Extend the tongue between the teeth.

6. *Snorting pigs:* Imitate the snorting of a pig with [ŋ]. Note the sensation at the bridge of the nose. Increase the frequency of the snorts, choosing lower and higher pitch patterns.

7. *Buzzing bees:* Bees buzz with [n], [m] or [ŋ]. [n] is used for nasal resonance, [m] for mouth resonance and [ŋ] for head resonance. Imagine the bees caught in the nose, creeping into the head. Follow their wanderings with a hand.

8. *Grumbling flies:* A fly is caught in a glass, or a jar or a barrel. The head could represent the container. The fly rises and falls. The buzzing sounds should rise and fall, too. Pretend that the fly is buzzing in a tunnel or in the bathtub or shower. Here again, the consonants [m], [n] and [ŋ] will be used.

c. To encourage consistency in the vocal registers

1. *Groaning or sighing:* Groan uncontrollably on *ng* [ŋ]. The tip of the tongue falls over the lower teeth. The eyes should be closed. Imagine the pain of a headache. The groaning sounds rise and fall, increase and decrease. Sense that the sound moves from the head to the throat and chest. The sound ascends, the bodily sensation descends and vice versa.

2. *Flying game:* A small plane flies overhead. It circles close to the earth and then sweeps upwards again. Imitate the sound of the approaching and departing plane. Begin softly, allowing the tone to grow and fade. A circu-

lar hand motion in front of the face may assist the imagination.

3. *Siren game:* Slide through the registers on the same continuing sounds *m*, *n*, and *ng* ([m], [n], [ŋ]) creating the sound of a police or ambulance siren.

4. *Ping-pong:*

aa. Speak and sing the syllable "ping" and "pong." Keep the vowel as short as possible. The consonant [p] explodes, simulating the sound of the bouncing ball.

bb. Sing the syllable substituting all the vowels.

cc. Move on to the exercises below, short vowel, long *ng* [ŋ].

The gliding motion of [ŋ] should carry the head resonance into the lower registers. Be careful that the tone does not fall into the throat. It may help to imagine the tones as drops of water on the nose, sliding down to the tip and dropping off. Point to the tone with a forefinger.

These exercises can also be sung on similar monosyllabic words such as "cling," "clang," "bing," "bang."

dd. Add words with mixed vowel sound combinations: "murmuring," "testing" (or "müde" as in the German language) for example.

During the repetitions of these words, drop the [ŋ] intermittently to check the placement of the vowels. The exercises described above are used as models. It is insignificant to which pitches the patterns are sung, but it is important to use comfortable ranges of the voice. After consistency and ease are achieved in the middle of the scale, exercises should venture to other areas of the voice.

ee. Sing these exercises on "when," "sam," "soon," or "whom" with an inquisitive attitude. The body opens for better resonance automatically.

The conductor should be alert always to any wrinkled brows or strained faces in the choir. Not only does a smiling face produce a freer, more resonant sound but also a brighter vowel sound. A tone which is brighter blends more easily in an ensemble setting. It is helpful to suggest a slight spreading of the nostrils, lifting the upper lip for more mouth space and better tonal placement.

d. Ways to avoid the Knödel (nodes), relax the throat and place the tone properly.

(The term 'Knödel' is literally translated 'dumpling' and denotes, in singing, the compression of the back of the tongue in the pharyngeal region. The Knödel blocks the vocal tract, causing pressure on the vocalis muscle during phonation. The resultant tone is constricted in quality and mobility).

1. *Goat game:* Group the singers in couples. The singers should face each other with foreheads pressed together. They can imitate the sounds of goats.

2. *Ramming the head through a wall:* Press the forehead against a wall and hum. Notice the sensation of resonance in the facial area.

3. *Sneezing:* Sneeze with a loud "hatschi!" Pretend that the sneeze is caught in a handkerchief. The second time, sneeze and extend the last syllable over many pitches. Then sneeze on other vowel sounds, for ex., "hatschu," or "hatscha," etc. ([u], [a]). Diaphragm impulses should be used under each syllable, first in speech and then in singing. The syllable "ha" [a] broadens the space at the back of the mouth and the consonants *tsch* [t ʃ] force the tone forward.

4. *First cry of a baby:* Groan quietly on [φ] or [æ]. The sound becomes more emphatic. Glide from above in pitch with a bright, nasal vowel. Finally the baby cries "äng" [εŋ]! The pitch fluctuates high and low as if an infant were wailing (Register consistency).

5. *Additional examples:*

aa. Many images create a *forward placement* of the voice: drops of water falling from the nose, the face of a ravenous animal, the puckered lips of a fish in a pond or an aquarium.

bb. Imagine a *fish* is gathering bread crumbs. Imagine the singing sound beginning between the eyes. The tone should not be pressed out like drops of juice from a lemon, but should spring from the lips by itself. Laughing is a good example of a well-placed sound.

cc. Imagine that the tone forms a *halo about the head.* Pull the tone out of the hair as if an electrical spark were nestled near the scalp.

dd. In developing exercises for *placement,* use the vowel [i] (closed i as in see) with [f], [m], [s], [v], [z], [d] and [b] as well as [n], [ng], or [m]. Sing the same patterns using the vowel [a].

e. Ways to open and strengthen the voice

The voice should be locked into place. These exercises are built on speech patterns in order to apply what has been learned to the singing of texts.

1. *Yawning:* It is always beneficial to use the yawn between other exercises. Yawning frees the voice and relaxes the body. Yawn quietly and follow the yawn with a sigh.

2. *Questions and answers:*

aa. The resonating cavities are opened, when a question is posed. The voice rises at the end of the phrase, placing the tone forward. Begin with a dark vowel on any pitch. Let the sound rise inquisitively. Select words of one or two syllables. The conductor speaks the words and the singers repeat them several times: for instance, "who?" "no?" why?" "what?" "when?" "how?" "see?"

bb. Divide the choir into two groups, one to ask the *questions* and the other to *answer.* The responses may be: "how?" "now!" "who?" "you!" "why?" "oh, my!" "what?" "that!" "when?" "then!" "see?" "we see!" The pitch of the questioning phrase rises and the response falls.

cc. Assign fixed pitches to the phrases. Use whole sentences as questions and answers, for ex.: "Have you seen Mary today?" "Yes, I saw Mary today." These sentences can be chanted and then sung.

dd. Next, choose *familiar songs* which begin with questions, such as: *Baa, baa, black sheep, have you any wool? Are you sleeping? Do you love me? Oh say, can you see?* Isolate the phrases with questions first. Speak the words as spoken phrases. Chant them on one pitch, allowing the pitch to rise at the end. Sing the phrase on any pattern of tones. Then sing the whole verse of the song. The open feeling created by the question should be maintained throughout the singing of the song.

3. *Astonishment and wonder:* The bodily sensation of openness to sound and resonance will be intensified with inner excitement. Burst forth with a cry of "oo!", "ah!" "aha!", "ohho!" Proceed as suggested above by selecting phrases and songs which have exclamatory passages, like: *Oh, what a beautiful morning! O Christmas tree!*

4. *Calling:* It is important to recognize the difference between a call and a scream. Calling encourages good vocal production while screaming hinders it. In daily life, one cannot avoid calling for someone or something at one time or another. It is part of a normal routine. Because it is a necessary mode of expression, the body supports the sound well without voluntary

assistance. Calling strengthens the voice and gives the pattern of speech a sense of direction. The tone has more carrying power or focus.

aa. The *telephone* rings. Answer with a calm "hello!" The caller does not reply. Repeat "hello" several times with increased antagonism. Form an imaginary receiver with the hands. Be sure that the consonant *l* is articulated with the tip of the tongue. Call out "hello" through cupped hands, as if beckoning for someone through a woods. Listen for an echo. Divide the choir into a calling and an echoing group.

bb. These *calls* can be varied at will. For example: "Hello, Taxi!"; "Hello, Waiter,!" and so on. A suitable gesture of the hand will help to enhance the effect. Choose exclamations which relate to different fields of experience: "ahoy,!", "gangway,!" (Sailors) or "fore!" (Golfers). Imitate a yodeler if possible. Each singer should call in his or her own manner.

cc. The sounds can be combined with specific pitches and tonal melodies. The last step is to choose songs with exclamatory phrases: like *Viva la musica!*

dd. *Calling names:* The mother calls her child to dinner. The children call to one another while playing. Call out the names of friends. Call the name of a child who is lost in the woods. Begin with names which contain darker vowel sounds. Advance progressively to lighter ones. A sample series follows: "Susan," "Morris," "Margaret," "Elaine," "Emile."

Most names do not have mixed vowel combinations. Invent a series of nonsense syllables using oy, [o i] ow, [o u] ay, [e i] aw, [a u] etc. Samples: "Roy!" "Howard!" "May!" "Maw!" and "Paw!" Names which contain [m], [n] or [ŋ] are especially useful for combining resonance and tonal placement. Consider such names as: "Tanya," "Samson," "Mignon."

ee. Call the names instinctively. Build the names into exercises as described above with questions, calls and exclamations. Arrange the names by vowel sound. Try to move from one vowel color to the next without altering the tone quality. Perhaps a mother would call her children together: "Beulah!" "Margo!" "Hannah!" "Martin!" "Rosemary!"

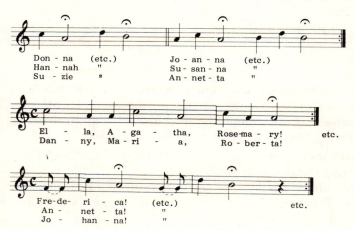

Jo - han - na! (etc.)
A - man - da! "
Ma - ri - a! "
An - ge - la!

Wan - da! (etc.)
Sam - son! "
In - grid! "
Kris - ten! "

An-na! (etc.)
Jan-na! "
Al-bert! "

(Until the ninth and back)

Al-len! (etc.)
El-la! "
Fran-cie! "

Char - lie!
Jen - ny!
Bet- ty!
Tom- my!

simile

Ot - to! Ot - to! Ot - to! Ot - to!
An - na! An - na! An - na! An - na!
Li- sa!
Jo-nah!
I- da!
A-my!

5. *Imitating the sounds animals make:* The same sort of activity has been mentioned above. The sounds animals utter are good examples of clear, natural tonal placement. Even though the uncultivated sound cannot be used directly in singing, the principle of focus can be applied.

aa. *Pigs:* Pigs wallow in the pen. The sounds uttered are "öng" [ɸŋ]. Guide the grunt from the diaphragm.

bb. *Cows:* The muted rumbling of contented cows is a clear example of good resonance. The sound becomes more intense, until a steady low-pitched "m" is heard and then "moo." [u]

cc. *Owl:* The owl flies and calls through the night. The suspense of the dark forest is heard in its call "who?" [u]

dd. *Dogs:* Imitate the barking of a dog. Note the activity in the abdominal region. Different breeds of dog have different kinds of barking sounds. Imagine a mad dog, a hungry dog, a wild dog, a puppy dog. Use "bow-wow!"

ee. *Cats:* Think of the syllable "meow" as if it were spelled [mɪɔu]. The *m* will aid in resonance, the *i* will draw the tone forward while the *o* relaxes and lowers the vocal mechanism. Repeat the sounds vigorously.

ff. *Donkey:* Repeat [ɪa] many times, sliding from one vowel to another.

gg. *Chicken:* Hammer out the syllables "gack-gack-gack" [gæk] pretending the chicken is clucking to gather her chicks about her. Then cluck as if the chicken were laying eggs.

hh. *Raven:* The "rab-rab" [rab] call should not be made in a crowing manner. Call the sound forth, rolling the *r* with the tip of the tongue.

ii. *Ducks:* The duck quacks "nat-nat" [nat]. The *n* opens the resonators. The [a] widens the space for the tone. The *t* consciously ends the flow of tone.

jj. *Sheep:* The sheep bleats "möh" [mø] and the lamb makes a "meh" [mɛ] sound.

kk. *Goats:* The nagging of a goat is heard as interrupted impulses. Use the diaphragm to make these pulsations: "mee" [me].

ll. *Rooster:* Do not make the "Cock-a-doodle-doo" in the throat. Glide downwards on the last syllable each time.

mm. *Chicks:* The choir could be a brood of chicks, each peeping at his or her own pace. The vowel sound will be heard continuously punctuated by the consonant *p*.

nn. *Horses:* The horse snorts a "ne" [nɪ] with impulses controlled by the diaphragm.

The animal calls should be made as authentically as possible. Move from these random calls to calls at definite pitch levels. Follow the same procedure as with the name calling exercises above.

6. *Songs which use animal sounds and calls:* Such songs should be used to reach the same goals as described above (see "Calling names," 4,ee). The use of familiar songs for voice training is advantageous. The choir is not aware of the work being done. Sung in unison, the melodies can reinforce the choral sound while establishing a pleasant atmosphere for more serious work. Calls can be improvised in a canonic fashion to help guide the group toward polyphonic singing. If a choral arrangement of a folk song or nursery rhyme exists, use it as a transition from the exercise to the regular repertoire. The conductor should use the songs carefully, indicating to the group the dual importance of them. Here are some songs which may be used: *Old MacDonald Had a Farm,* or *Git Along Home, Little Doggies, Three Little Kittens, Cock a Doodle Doo, My Maid Has Lost Her Shoe, Ole King Cole.*

In a call, clear enunciation of each syllable is inherent.

aa. *Secular examples: Sour Wood Mountain,* patriotic songs like *Columbia, the Gem of the Ocean; God Bless America; The Battle Hymn of the Republic;* negro spirituals like *Go Tell It on the Mountain, De Gospel Train.*

bb. *Sacred examples: Hallelujah Amen, Michael Row the Boat Ashore, The Palms.*

cc. *Examples in children's songs:* Songs which imitate instruments or other objects *The Orchestra; Hickory Dickory, Dock; A Hunting we will go.*

dd. *Canons using calling sounds:* As with songs, canons can be used effectively. The canon has the added feature of harmonic movement, rhythmic and tonal interest. These elements lead directly to attentive, artistic music-making. Examples of canons with laughing refrains were listed above. In addition, try *Row, Row Your Boat; Brother John, etc.*

7. *Exercises to relax and activate the tongue:* The dog has run a long way. He arrives home with his tongue hanging out of his mouth. The tongue lies flat and rests its weight on the jaw. Try to stretch the tip of the tongue up to touch the nose. Moisten the lips with the tongue. Count all of the teeth in the mouth with the tongue. Flutter the tongue between the lips. Sing cannons or folk songs with *tra-la-la* or *fa-la-la* refrains. The tip of the tongue articulates the *l* with quick, clear motions.

8. *Exercises for relaxing the lips:* Whistle a tune or a canon. Pretend to play a flute, puckering the lips over the mouthpiece. Half of the choir could sing a song about the springtime, while the other half replies with bird calls. Whistling uses the lips actively. Speak and sing words with the vowels [u] and [i] one after another. This will loosen the lips and face muscles. Choose nicknames like: "Lucy," "Suzi," "Muti." A chain of nicknames can be used in the same way as described above under the heading "Calling names," (4,ee). Pluck fruit of various sizes from the vine with the lips. Grab for the fruit with a particular vowel sound in mind, for example, cherries [u], plums [o] and apples [a]. A rounded mouth opening (fishmouth) is important for achieving a consistent vowel formation within the context of a choral sound.

IV. USE OF VOICE TRAINING IN A CHOIR REHEARSAL

Few conductors would wish to use all of the above mentioned exercises in choir rehearsals. Most conductors choose a time at the beginning or in the middle of the rehearsal for warm-up exercises. There are some choirs which would not be willing to spend time on voice building. For this reason, the conductor must be clever and creative in delivering the exercises at the appropriate moment: as an opening or closing song, as syllables for rehearsing a work, as aids for managing the language, etc. It would be most desirable to devote ten to fifteen minutes at the beginning of the rehearsal to warm-ups. Here are three examples of ways to organize warm-up periods:

a. Voice training for a specific problem

An enthusiastic conductor conducts a willing choir. The singers understand the necessity of proper training for their voices. In this case, the conductor has the opportunity to plan a series of exercises addressing the various areas of voice building.

1. *The conductor has a group of singers with limited ability and training.* The majority cannot read music. The singers come together after a busy day at their respective jobs. They must be calmed and drawn together before the rehearsal can begin. A familiar song can be sung in unison. The song should contain useful syllables (see IV, e, 5-6). To support the singers and to heighten the musical experience, the conductor may add an accompanying instrument: piano, organ, trumpet, trombone, violin or recorders—even an accordion. The instrument may play the accompaniment, the melody or a freely-improvised descant. The song should be changed with the seasons of the year, or if the song is a hymn, for the periods of the liturgical year.

The conductor allows the sounds to be formed in a natural way. The melody from a work to be studied may be chosen. The melody can be sung on a syllable which predominates in the text of the work. Singing the work on a homogenous syllable helps to mold the choral sound. Next, the group is asked to clap the rhythm of the melody. This rhythmic pattern is repeated on [f] pulsations to relax and activate the diaphragm. To promote steady exhalations, the exercise for cooling the soup (II,b,2) can be used. Exercises must follow which loosen the vocal and breathing mechanisms. These would include groaning on [n], [ŋ] or [m] (III,a,4). For breath support, play the locomotive games. Puff off the stream as explained for II,a,Iaa.

A portion of the work to be studied will be introduced on a single syllable. This binds the warm-ups to the rehearsal itself. If voice building began with a melody from the work, use that melody here to conclude the warm-ups.

2. *The conductor has a choir of singers who are very restless.* It is difficult for the conductor to maintain the choir's concentration. The conductor should wait until all the singers are absolutely quiet. Nothing happens for a few moments. Allow the singers to sit comfortably on their chairs. Their arms hang loosely. They drop their heads on their chests and close their eyes, completely relaxed. The ensuing stillness will be broken with light, easy groaning on [ŋ] or an indistinct grumbling sound. The conductor speaks softly. Use the down feather exercise (II,b,5) for exhalation. Follow with the exercise described in II,c,7, wherein a football is inflated.

An active group like this one should respond well to laughing games. Grunting can be introduced for resonance (III,a,1). Groaning on a gliding [ŋ] will assist the resonators and unify the vocal registers (also III,b,6 and III,c,1).

The baby's first cry (as explained in III,d,4) brings the voice to its proper placement. Hearty yawning broadens the space for the tone in the body and sets up a better connection between the resonators and the breath support (III,e,1). Calling in various forms strengthens the voice and establishes good vocal production (III,4). A canon on specific syllables or a laughing canon can complete the voice training. It is possible, of course, to use sections of the work to be studied, to which laughing or calling syllables may be added. This will coordinate the training sessions with the rehearsal to follow.

b. Voice training dealing with the specific vocal technical problems of the choir

A conductor recognizes the vocal deficiencies of the singers. It is clear where the difficulties lie. The conductor will want to work on these problems from one session to another.

1. *The choir does not produce a good choral sound.* The tone is breathy and flaccid. It cannot be amplified or diminished. The choral sound does not project. This might be more prevalent in a youth choir or girls' ensemble. The reason for all of these problems is inadequate support of the tone. Air is escaping which is not used in tone. The tone is not focused, because the resonators are not being properly used. There is no strength among the singers.

Emphasis should be placed on breath support and control. Movement exercises should be used for the hips and diaphragm, for example: churning butter, climbing, throwing stones, cutting grass, chopping wood (I,a). For exhalation, ask the singers to blow against a frozen window (II,b,1). The hunting game with "piff," "puff," "poof" and the horse games would be helpful also (II,a,3).

The singers breathe out and count their heart beats thereby. The length of time for holding the breath should be increased. It is important that the singers wait for the breath to come by itself. To aid in proper breath management, use the exercises for surprise and astonishment (described in II,c,3). Then the singer works through a familiar children's song with diaphragmatic pulsations on [f] (II,c,4). Use the buzzing of flies caught in a jar (III,b,8) with [m], [n], [ŋ] to build resonance. The flies break out of the jar and fly around the room. Follow them with a finger, guiding the breath and the voice at the same time. In order to bring more focus to the tone, different kinds of laughing can be suggested (II,a,I,ee). Perhaps a canon with laughing figures would help. To develop more sound, work with calling patterns (III,e,4,dd) and the other exercises associated with them. By repeating the syllables again and again, the concept is reinforced for the singer. Example: The name "Samson" will be stuttered "sam-sam-sam-samson!" Pluck fruit from the vine with the fishmouth form on the lips (III,e)! Laughing and name calling games will complete the voice training for this session.

2. *The choir sings too loud;* (in fact, it screams). The sound is hard and inflexible, so that there is no musical line. The choral sound is out of tune

and does not project acoustically. This could be the case with a men's ensemble.

The basic problem may be too much muscular pressure on the voices. The singers force the air and thus the tone. They probably breathe too often. When the throat is constricted, a raw sound is produced. All of the vocal mechanism is in a state of tension. The singers are physically and psychologically cramped.

A complete stillness must be commanded by the conductor. Each singer should be as quiet and as content as possible. Ask each singer to pretend to fall asleep in a chair with a loosened jaw (III,b,2,3). It would be helpful if gymnastic exercises could be practiced such as shaking the limbs, nodding the head, waving in various ways, rolling the head and shoulders, swinging and swaying the entire body (I,a,b).

Sighing and yawning will relax the singer (II, Introduction). Special attention should be given to see that the singer uses all of the breath conservatively with exercises such as horse games, puffing dandelions, etc. (as in II,b,4). See also the exercises which are suggested for holding the breath, for example: listening in the dark woods, bringing a crowd to silence (II,c,8). In the atmosphere of quiet, the conductor may whisper so that the singers listen breathlessly. Burping and hiccuping will activate the diaphragm, conserve the air, and allow for better inhalation. (II,a,4). Mosquitoes humming in the peaceful summer night could be imitated, using a hushed *s* [s]. This helps guide the air flow. Stuttering with fricative or explosive syllables (II,b,8) helps breath support. The humming of bees builds resonance (II,c,9). Choose a children's song with a humming passage in it. Be careful that the singing remains at a relaxed dynamic level. The exercises using the air pump should be avoided. (The singers breathe out all of their unused air at the end of each phrase.) The conductor insists that no one breathes during a phrase. After each phrase, the air should be expelled as if controlled by a valve.

To avoid the cramped Knödel (constricted tongue) syndrome, try the exercise for ramming the head through the wall (III,d,2). The yawn and sneeze exercises are worthwhile for the same purpose, i.e., building resonance. It is essential that an intense, high forward placement of the voice be developed (III,d,3). The exercises for loosening the tongue (II,d,5,cc,dd) are also needed.

To develop the choral sound, select suitable animal sounds which are relaxed and meditative—the mooing of the cow, the meowing of the cat. Sing through the choral piece on one of these syllables. Then advancing to mixed polyphonic works, try first a canon such as *Row, Row, Row Your Boat* sung with dark vowel sounds ([u] [o] [œ]). Each singer must listen to the sound of the entire group. Tuning exercises may be needed to develop this awareness. (Ehmann, *Choral Directing*, pp. 65ff.) Also, songs with echoes in them can be sung. The conductor should sing or play a phrase loudly and ask the choir to sing it back as an echo.

c. Voice training in preparation for the choral repertoire

Perhaps the choir and its conductor are accustomed to training the voice as described here. Above the basic vocal technical skills which can be developed in warm-ups, specific problems from the choral literature can be tackled separately:

1. *Take, for instance, a work which is humorous in character.* Often the tessitura of such a work will be especially high for singers. Begin with relaxation and posture exercises, perhaps ball games, plucking fruit, balancing on a curb (I,a,b). To increase a feeling for the body and to activate the breathing muscles, follow with hopping, skipping and humming. Then smell a wonderful bouquet of fragrant spring flowers, or taste a ripe peach which makes the mouth water (II, Introduction). The machine gun games and train games will loosen the diaphragm and compress the air (II,a,2,5). The games for cooling hot foods and balancing the celluloid ball help with steady and guided exhalation (II,b,3,5). The exercises (II,e,3) depicting shock assist in breath management.

When developing breath support, laughing exercises should not be forgotten, particularly for flexible staccato singing of various patterns of rhythmic and poetic stress. (III,a,I,bb). Vary the kind of laughing from general frivolity to the uninhibited giggling of children (III,a,I,dd). Children's songs and dances will work with laughing syllables. The imitation of sheep (III,b,5) loosens the jaw. Humming in the bathtub and in a tunnel add resonance (III,b,8) and the pilot game will solidify the vocal registers (III,c,2). To achieve high, forward placement of the voice, use the pacemaker exercise (III,d,5,cc,dd) with short syllables of bright and dark vowels. To increase the resonating space, open the sound and insure placement, the calling exercises (from III,e,4,bb) are recommended. The exercise in name calling will free the high voice (III,e,4,dd,ee). Move slowly upwards, first stepwise and then in triads. The use of mixed and umlaut vowels is very important. Never allow the singers to frown. Work for flexible management of the language of the song.

The tone syllables which were used methodically until now should be organized as they appear in the song text. Hence, the singer has an open door to applying the warm-up exercise to the repertoire.

2. *The choral work to be studied is solemn in character;* the tempo is *grave.* The voices must sing passages in the lowest portion of their ranges.

Begin with exercises which cause the body to bound and swing, for example: standing on tiptoe, ringing bells, chopping wood, making circles with the arms. A sweeping feeling is essential (I,a,b). A canon with bells might begin the rehearsal (*Brother John,* for example.)

For steady, relaxed breath support, yawning and groaning should take place (II, Introduction). Breathing against a frozen window helps regular, thorough exhalation (II,b,I). Play the games with the bicycle tire or with the steam engine (II,a,5,b,6). The relaxed and patient waiting for air is extremely important. Listen breathlessly to a whispered secret which is told in detail. Diving exercises strengthen breath support, also (II,c,5).

For building the voice, work primarily with dark sounds and a string of laughing syllables pulsated on "hoo" [u] or "ho" [o] (II,a,hh). The jaw should hang as if the singer had fallen asleep (III,b,c). The resonators will be needed for focusing the voice. Perhaps the singers will find the bee exercises helpful. The ping-pong game with its related exercises (III,c,4,cc) are indispensable. Move stepwise into the lower range at a quiet dynamic. The tones should be imagined as drops of water on the nose in order for the head resonance and the lower register to be combined. The goat games and their accompanying images are useful for the proper placement of the voice (III,d,1-5). Reinforce the proper placement of the tone through exercises which use the question or exclamation (III,b,1-3). Be attentive to the musical phrase when forming the exercises. The sound should be rounded and the tone progressions, even (III,e,8). Check the directions for staggering the breath (see Ehmann, *Choral Directing* pp. 15ff). A slow, solemn canon can be sung to bridge the gap between the warm-ups and the rehearsal, for example: *Hi-ho, Anybody Home?*

Begin with dark vowel syllables. All the texts should be recited on one tone before being applied to the melodies.

Chapter B

PRACTICAL EXERCISES IN CHORAL VOICE BUILDING BASED UPON THE PRINCIPLES SET FORTH IN CHAPTER A

Often one encounters a choral conductor who begins each rehearsal with two or three standard vocalises every week throughout the year. This kind of warm-up may not harm the choir, but it probably does not help it either. The singers need not concentrate to sing the familiar scale patterns. Some may arrive ten minutes late to the rehearsal in order to avoid the warm-up period altogether. The choral conductor believes that the responsibility to the choir is fulfilled by giving it this brief opportunity to exercise, and proceeds immediately to the main assignment: namely, learning the notes of the music. Hence the voices are treated as if they were man-made instruments, when in actuality many voices rely solely on the choral experience for their development. The choral conductor becomes the voice instructor as well as the musical leader of the group.

An orchestral conductor assumes that every orchestra member has been trained to play the instrument he holds. Thus the conductor dictates the bowing to the string players. Economical use of rehearsal time with the brass players protects embouchures. Union rules require that frequent breaks be given to allow musicians sufficient rest. The amateur choir member, on the other hand, must sing for as many as two hours at a time, seldom moving from the seat. Facilities for choral rehearsals are rarely adequate. Under most circumstances, the amateur is asked to repeat one difficult passage after another, many of which demand technical skills beyond the comprehension of the untrained singer.

Textbooks which imply that a clear conducting pattern permits the conductor access to a choir or orchestra are short-sighted. An established conducting technique is necessary to a choral conductor, but the conductor should not forget that the hands are useless if they do not speak to the needs of the singer. Therefore, the conductor's movements indicate the vocal language the singers will translate into well-formed sounds.

Since the voice is the "instrument" upon which the choral conductor plays, understanding its structure and its function is most important. Words and actions must support good vocal habits. If the conductor is capable of incorporating this concept into choral work, one can create an artistic instrument from the collection of voices in a choir. Thus the choral masterworks can be prepared with a minimum of time, effort and vocal strain.

To illustrate this point, we offer two examples: The sopranos of the choir sing an entire passage repeatedly under the pitch. If the conductor does not recognize the reason for the intonation problems, badgering the singers with "sing higher" usually results. The phrase can be sung again and again until it is sung in tune. The conductor could have saved time, nervous energy and vocal fatigue by realizing the vocal problem involved. The intonation may have been faulty because the high voices were giving too much chest sound to the vowel 'ae' [ɛ]. By modifying the vowel to 'eh' [e] or 'e' [ɪ], the chest quality will be transformed to a brighter head sound. After singing the phrase on one of these brighter vowels, the singers will adjust instinctively to a higher placement of the voice when singing the phrase with the text.

Another example: The choir does not articulate the text clearly. The tiresome command "pronounce the words" proves useless. A short exercise can be employed. Pant like a dog (draw attention to diaphragmatic support). Use explosive consonants articulated from the center of the body with light diaphragmatic pressures: 'p', 't', 'k', 'ss', 'tsch' (to strengthen the breath musculature). Next, select a phrase of text from the work. Practice the phrase with the consonants 'p', 't', 'k', 'ss', 'tsch'. Divide the syllables of the text with quarter-note rests. Speak the line of text, exaggerating the consonants. Sing the line at one pitch level and then as written. (See CII,a,9).

Technical helps presented in this manner spark the interest of the singer to whom vocal technique as such, seems superfluous.

The choral conductor should organize a plan of development for the singers, approaching each of the major areas of voice building systematically:

Blending the sound
Dynamics
High and low
Intonation
Language
Elimination of extraneous sounds

This list will be expanded to accommodate the difficulties which arise in choral literature:

Legato
Staccato
Martellato
Accents and sforzati
Crescendo and decrescendo
ppp to fff
Vowel modification
Attack on open vowels
Agility
Clear diction

I. EXERCISES BUILT UPON THE EXAMPLES GIVEN IN CHAPTER A

The following exercises deal with the structure and function of the singer's "instrument:"

Body and mind relaxation
Posture
Breathing mechanism as instigator
Vocal tract as producer of tone
Resonance as amplifier of the tone

a. Relaxation exercises (See A I,a-c)

Additions:

1. Ask the singers to massage the back and shoulders of their neighbors.

2. Lift the right shoulder as high as the ear and let it fall with a heavy arm. Do the same with the left shoulder and then with both shoulders at the same time. Breathe normally—not in the rhythm of the shoulder movements! Turn the shoulders backward and forward in big circular motions.

3. Roll the head slowly as if it were a big apple on a thin stem; reverse the direction.

4. Drop the head to one side and then carry it over to the other side and let it "fall down." Next, drop the head forward and pull it up and back.

5. Stretch, yawn and sigh freely.

b. Posture exercises (See A I,b)

Additions:

1. Carry a cake on each shoulder. Move cautiously, so as not to drop the cakes.

2. Balance a basket of fruit on the head.

3. Each singer pretends to be a lighthouse. Only the head turns as if the eyes were casting a beam of light.

4. Fall forward from the waist, shaking the air from the hanging arms; gradually return the body to an upright position by lifting one vertebra after another. Breathe in and out passively.

5. Lean against a wall so that every inch of the backbone touches the wall. Ease the body away from the wall by slipping the feet forward and slide them back again. Retain erect posture. Allow even the shoulders to touch the wall.

6. While seated, measure the area between the navel and the epigastrium with the span of a hand. By doing this, a singer can obtain a good sitting posture for singing. If the conductor notices a choir of slouching bodies during a rehearsal, choir members should be asked to measure their posture, using this method.

c. Relaxation of the diaphram exercises (See A II,a,1-5)

Additions:

1. aa. With the tongue wagging out of the mouth, pant like a dog after a long, hot walk. Begin in a slow tempo and steadily increase momentum. Place a hand on the abdomen to feel the diaphragmatic response.

bb. Using the same panting action, speak the following consonants: 'h', 'f', 'h', 'f', 'h', 'f' [h] [f]. Then substitute diaphragm pushes for the panting and speak:

> 'p', 't', 'k' [p] [t] [k]
> 'f', 'ss', 'tsh' [f] [s] [t ʃ]
> 'rrr' or 'br', 'br' [r] ⌊br⌋

cc. Use consonants in various patterns to increase the choir's power of concentration. NOTE: Never begin at a rapid speed. Choose a tempo at which each consonant can be articulated clearly.

2. aa. The conductor can chant a series of consonants in different rhythmic configurations. The choir imitates the conductor's demonstration exactly. Be sure to form the consonants accurately with the lips and tongue. Perform the diaphragm pushes vigorously. Allow no motion in the chest and shoulders.

bb. Choose the rhythm of a familiar song such as: *The Star Spangled Banner;* or *Row, Row, Row your Boat.* Divide the choir into four groups, assigning each group a consonant. For example: 's' [s], 'p' [p], 't' [t], 'tsh' [t ʃ]. The conductor or the singers may improvise individual rhythmic figures also.

d. Exhalation exercises (See A II,b,1-8)

Additions:

1. Whisper an exclamatory phrase: *Oh, what a beautiful morning!; Joy to the world!; My Lord, what a morning!; It's almost like being in love!; Lo, how a rose e're blooming!*

If these exclamations are made in a pianissimo dynamic, the diaphragm remains passive. When the phrases are repeated fortissimo, the immediate diaphragmatic involvement can be felt in the abdomen, sides and back.

2. The singers breathe as if they were asleep. Allow them to slouch on their chairs with their eyes closed. Ask them to exhale vigorously through a slightly open mouth and then pause for a brief interval before inhaling quickly through the nose with the mouth open. After exhaling, the singers sigh. This exercise calms a nervous choir and brings an air of concentration to the rehearsal. The singers experience the advantages of intense exhalation. Note the importance of the interval between exhalation and inhalation. The body will cry out for breath when it is needed. After three or four cycles of breath, place a hand on the abdominal muscles with the fingers extended between the navel and the epigastrium. The other hand should check the region between the ribs and the spinal column to insure total support (diaphragmatic-intercostal breathing).

3. Create a wind with streams of breath, using the consonant 'f'. First make a light breeze and increase to a heavy storm wind. Use the hands to indicate the direction of the air currents.

e. Inhalation and support exercises (See A II,c,1-9)

Additions:

1. Imagine a floor under the lungs. The air of inhalation must lower the floor to allow a place for the air to rest. If the singer thinks vertically and not horizontally, the abdominal muscles under the navel will guide the air upwards with a sense of expansion. This motion is not hectic but energetic.

2. With an imaginary drinking straw between the lips, blow out air in three blasts. Wait a moment and draw air through the straw in three gulps. It is helpful to imagine that the legs are two "pipes" through which one can draw the air from the floor to the waistline. Do not associate the lungs with breathing at all. Be careful not to disturb the placement of the shoulders and chest. Gradually increase the number of blasts and gulps from 3 to 6.

3. The following image will help the breath without straining the vocal tract: The singer pretends there are four noses attached about the belt through which breath can be drawn directly to the abdominal area. Imagine more noses (up to 8). (Nasal breathing with the mouth partially open).

4. It is possible to achieve a guide for the breath low in the body by closing one nostril while inhaling. The sensation of inhalation is more intense and directional.

5. Breath support must include the muscles of the back. Raise the arms to shoulder height. Blow out all air on 'f' [f], wait a moment and sip the air into the body on 'f' [f]. Roll the arms backward until the thumbs point behind the body. Turn the arms forward and exhale—sigh—relax—repeat.

6. The depth of breath intake will be increased when one inhales through the vowel 'u' [u]. Exhale on the consonant 'f' [f] with the mouth in a fishmouth position. Wait a moment, maintain the position of the mouth and imagine the inner feeling of the 'u' [u] vowel as the air escapes. Inhale again.

Repeat this exercise until the breath is well anchored. Each vowel activates another area of the breath mechanism because each vowel resides in its own resonating region:

[u] lower abdomen under the rib cage
[o] middle of rib cage
[a] chest area
[e] pharynx
[i] head

One must remember to round the mouth when brightening the vowel.

7. The sensation of support during inhalation can be increased by imagining that the spinal column stretches as the air enters the lungs.

8. Sighing is used throughout this book to bring relaxation to the entire

body. It is recommended especially as an addition to any series of breath support exercises. During a choir rehearsal, ask the choir to sigh occasionally. Vary the vowel sounds to promote easy movement between the vocal registers (See B I,k,5).

f. Expanding the vocal tract exercises (See A III,e,1-4)

Additions:

1. Imagine that the jaw is filled with heavy metal. The mouth cannot hold it. The jaw drops open.

2. Attach an imaginary crayon to the jaw. Draw a circle with the crayon using the jaw to sketch the lines. The jaw should be relaxed. The facial expression will be flaccid and dumb. Be sure to round the lips.

3. aa. For relaxation, repeat the following syllables:
wa-wa-wa [va]; bla-bla-bla; fra-fra-fra; ga-ga-ga; na-na-na; tadada-tadada-tadada; kaga-kaga-kaga; scha-scha-scha [ʃa]. ·

bb. Sing these syllables on one pitch, or on the following exercises:

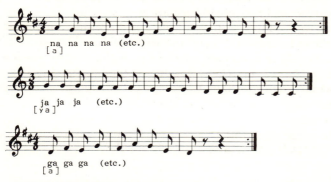

g. Relaxation of the tongue

Articulation Exercises (See A III,e,9).
Additions:

1. Rest the tongue against the upper lip as if the tongue were made of thin dough. Return it to its normal position behind the lower teeth. The jaw hangs by its own weight, completely relaxed. Repeat.

2. aa. Extend the tongue and retract as if one were imitating a poisonous snake. This exercise activates the tip of the tongue.

bb. Hold the jaw with a hand and speak rapidly 'la-la-la' [la] using only the tip of the tongue to articulate the consonants.

cc. Slide up and down on an 'r' [r] rolled with the tip of the tongue. Firm breath support makes the exercise possible.

dd. Sing the following passage on 'r' [r]:

ḡg.

hh.

ii.

3. Application of resonance to vowel formation:

The easiest way to combine resonance with vowel sounds is to create exercises which use the consonant 'l' [l] and the vowel 'u' [u]. The vowel 'u' [u] is audible when the 'l' [l] is formed by the tip of the tongue resting against the upper teeth. A "fishmouth" formation of the lips enhances the success of this exercise. It is important to note the deep position of the larynx inherent in the singing of the 'u' [u] vowel:

4. aa. Substitute other consonants for the 'l' [l]. Begin each exercise with the 'l' [l] as a point of reference. Advance chromatically in either direction. Shift from vowel to consonant with minimal tongue motion:

bb. For a next step toward focus, use the umlaut 'ü' [y] in combination with 'i' [i]. Note: The consonant comes before each beat:

cc. Apply the sensation of forward placement to other vowels. Be careful not to open the mouth excessively for 'a' [a] and ä [ɛ]. 'u' [u] remains the key for opening the "door" to resonance because it consists in high resonance and low larynx positions:

| lu | lo | lö | le | lu |
| [u] | [o] | [ø] | [e] | [u] |

| lu | lo | la | lä | lu |
| [u] | [o] | [a] | [ɛ] | [u] |

5. Move next to agility exercises based on the sustained consonants interrupted by vowels. This procedure promotes complete closure of the vocal folds—an essential element for good resonance:

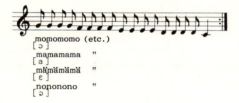

momomomo (etc.)
[ɔ]
mamamama   "
[a]
mämämämä   "
[ɛ]
nononono   "
[ɔ]

6. aa. Begin all resonance exercises in piano dynamic and develop a feeling within the singer for the emergence of sound from the body without effort. The facial muscles must be relaxed. Ask the choir members to close their eyes and enjoy the sound of their voices:

din-ge don-ge din-ge don-ge ding
[I][ə] [ɔ][ə]

bb.

min-ge mun-ge men-ge   mong mong mong
[I][ə][ʌ][ə][ɛ]   [ɔ]

7. aa. Use of names or terms with sustaining syllables:

sa - ving sa - ving (etc.)		sa -	ving
sing - ing sing - ing "		sing -	ing
ping pong ping pong "		ping	pong

ee. Sing an entire folk song on 'r'. Select a melody of limited range: Example: *The Water is Wide; Black Is The Color of My True Love's Hair; I Wonder As I Wander.*

3. Try to touch the tongue to the nose or to the chin.

4. Massage the back of the tongue by speaking a chain of vowel sounds. The tongue and lips should remain as stationary as possible so that the root of the tongue forms the vowels.

'ue' [ʏ]   'u' [u]

'a' [a]   'eh' [ɛ]   'e' [i]

h. Exercises for relaxation of the lips (See A III,e,8)

Additions:

1. aa. Vibration of the lips with 'b' (like a disgusted horse) loosens the lips and engages the diaphragm. Begin without a definite pitch then move freely up and down. Then sing:

bb.

cc.

dd.

ee.

i. Massaging the soft palate (See A III,e,6.aa)

Exercises for the articulators:

1. When a swan is upset, he rustles his wings and shrieks like a falcon 'ch' [ç]. Imitate this throaty sound.

2. Snore serenely (only while inhaling), with a loose jaw. The soft palate will flutter longer and louder the more relaxed it is.

3. Try snoring during exhalation as well. This activity is difficult. Only an isolated portion of the palate is used.

4. Repeat a lively parlando passage:

ka-ga-ka-ga-ka-ga [a]

j. Awakening the resonators (See A III,b,1-8; A III,e,5.aa-oo)

Work with the resonators connotes work with the registers of the voice. Breath support and expansion of the vocal tract should be taught before approaching the subject of resonance. The resonators must not be isolated from one another. Each resonating area cooperates with others to balance the spectrum of colors available to the voice. The highest tones of the range must have a certain percentage of chest resonance and chest tones need a point of focus in the head. Experience has shown that amateurs and beginners respond quickly to so-called "mask-resonance." When resonance is achieved within the "mask" of the face, the tone is free and well-focused.

Additions:

1. aa. Relax the jaw backwards. Rest the lips gently on each other as if they were very thick. Allow as much room in the mouth as possible by parting the teeth slightly. Hum at a low, comfortable pitch level. Imagine a tantalizing smell. To encourage forward placement of the sound, shape the mouth in a fishmouth form.

    bb. Avoid pressing the lips together. Sing 'hm' whereby the lips will vibrate. In this exercise, exhalation occurs through the nose and mouth simultaneously assuring good focus.

    cc. Place the hands in front of the face and hum into them. Guide the sound upward.

hm

2. aa. Repeat the exercises of 1., using other sustained consonants:
    'n' [n], 'ng' [ŋ], 'v' [v], 'l' [l]

    bb. To insure forward placement, sigh lightly on 'u' [u]. Glide from the vowel sound to a sustained consonant. Always check the jaw to be sure that the area surrounding the base of the tongue and throat is free from tension:

Advance to tonal exercises.

    cc. Glissando (descending direction):

    dd. Fixed pitches:

    ee.

    ff. Reverse the direction.

bb.

mam - ma	mi - a	mam - ma	mi - a
much more	mo - ney	much more	mo - ney
Son - ja	Son - ja	Son - ja	Son - ja

cc.

nja   nja   nja   (etc.)
[nja]

dd. The singers will notice the various locations for the placement of vowels and consonants in the following exercises:

sun-ny sun-ny (etc.)
bun-ny bun-ny "
bon-nie bon-nie "

ee.

sum - mer sum- mer (etc.)
ham - mer ham - mer "

8. aa. Resonance exercises are most helpful when applied to a chord or canon. A succession of vowels, for example: 'u' [u], 'a' [a], 'u' [u] creates a crescendo-decrescendo by increasing and decreasing the space within the mouth. Besides adding interest to the warm-up session, such choral vocalises can be used to check the tuning skills of the ensemble. The chords should be transposed by conjunct intervallic steps:

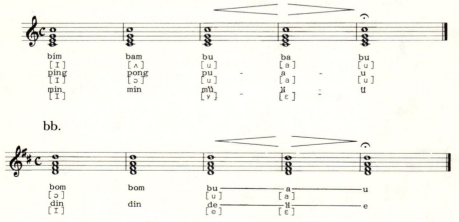

bim	bam	bu	ba	bu
[ɪ]	[ʌ]	[u]	[a]	[u]
ping	pong	pu -	a -	u
[ɪ]	[ɔ]	[u]	[a]	[u]
min	min	mü	ü -	u
[ɪ]		[y]	[ɛ]	

bb.

bom	bom	bu————a————u
[ɔ]		[u] [a]
din	din	de————ü————e
[ɪ]		[e] [ɛ]

9. Sing a canon, dividing each group by contrasting vowel sounds:

Example: Group 1 = bum, [ʊ], bum, bum
          Group 2 = bim, [ɪ], bim, bim
          Group 3 = böm, [œ], böm, böm
          Group 4 = bam, [ʌ], bam, bam

When Jesus Wept, William Billings

The vowel will be clipped while the consonants are sustained to maintain resonance and line. Each group sings the canon on the syllables indicated above. During the repetition of the canon, the consonants will be eliminated and the chain of vowels sustained:

                    Group 1 = bum [ʊ], bu [u], bum, bu, bum, bu
                    Group 2 = bim [ɪ], bi [i], bim, bi, bim, bi
                    Group 3 = böm [œ], bö [ø], böm, bö, böm, bö
                    Group 4 = bam [ʌ], ba [a], bam, ba, bam, ba

10. aa. As resonance unfolds, the voice takes on its actual character, its identity, its "timbre," its warmth and spirit. This individuality occurs when the edges of the vocal folds vibrate in cooperation with the nasal resonating cavities in piano dynamic. The singer couples the mask to the body using the skull as its resonating "roof." If the sound is a dark, covered sound, it is recommended that one use the nasal vowel indicative of the French language to combine nose, mouth and pharyngeal space. The tongue rests on the floor of the mouth, in the same position that is held for the 'ng' [ŋ] of the German language:

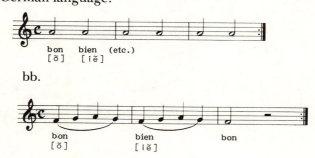

cc.

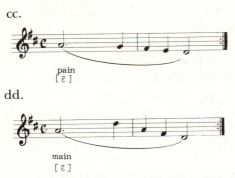

pain
[ɛ̃]

dd.

main
[ɛ̃]

ee. Substitute bright vowel sounds. It is helpful to round the lips (fishmouth) exposing the upper teeth slightly, ("rabbit-teeth"). The singer may wish to place a thumb behind the front teeth or the index finger under the nose to direct the sound outwards:

bien   be   (etc.)
[ɛ̃]   [e]

ff.

simile

main __ mü __   main __   me __(etc.)
[ɛ̃]   [ʏ]   [e]

gg.

pain _____   pe _____
[ɛ̃]   [e]

hh.

bien bon   bien ____   be
[ɛ̃] [ɔ̃]   [e]
bien bon   bien   ba
[ɛ̃]

ii. The high placement of brighter vowel formants will be transferred to darker vowel formants:

bien _____ bien _____   be — a _____
[ɛ̃]   [e]   [a]
main _____ mon _____   mu — o
[ɛ̃]   [o]   [u]   [o]

jj.

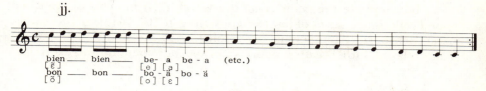

bien —— bien —— be- a be - a (etc.)
[ɛ̃]   [e] [a]
bon —— bon —— bo - ä bo - ä
[õ]   [o] [ɛ]

It is not necessary to suggest additional exercises for cultivating chest resonance. A singer who understands good breath control is able to produce sound by increasing pharyngeal space and by employing diaphragmatic support these elements being the basis for resonate singing. One can feel the throat opening in the following exercises: Imitate the hooting of an owl "hoo-hoo" [u] with the hands rounded about the mouth. Sigh heavily and deeply on the vowel 'u' [u].

k. Consistency of registers (See A III,c,1-4)

Additions:

1. aa. Vowel modification unites the registers and the resonators. The umlaut vowel combinations 'ue' [y], 'oe' [ø], 'ae' [ɛ] are especially helpful because they engage two resonating areas at once, i.e., the low laryngeal position of 'u' [u] with the high placement of 'i' [i]:

ü —— ü —— ü ——
[y]
ö —— ö —— ö ——
[ø]
ä —— ä —— ä ——
[ɛ]

bb.

ü —— ü —— ü —— ü
[y]
ö —— ö —— ö —— ö
[ø]

cc.

p ü —— u —— u ——
[y]
ö —— ö —— ö ——
[ø]
ä —— ä —— ä ——
[ɛ]

2. aa. To foster self-confidence in the singer's growth, suggest a yodeling exercise wherein register shifts are an intrinsic element:

dui du dui du dui du
[ui] [u]

bb. Suppose the choir sings the vowel 'i' [i] in a brassy, pinched manner. Present a series of low exercises using 'u' [u], 'a' [a], 'o' [o] vowels. Ascend chromatically opening the resonators to the sound. The jaw remains relaxed. Firm breath support is a prime ingredient for this exercise:

dua du   dua du   dua du
[ua][u]

cc.

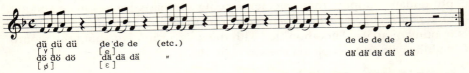

dü dü dü   de ˙de de   (etc.)   de de de de de
[y]   [e]
dö dö dö   dä dä dä   "   dä dä dä dä dä
[ø]   [ɛ]

dd. Sneezing is an unconscious act of the vocal registers. Sneeze intensely "hatschi." The diaphragm reacts immediately. Carry the sneezing sound down in a glissando as shown:

Ha—tschiii
[tʃi]

The frontal focus of the 'i' [i] vowel should be maintained in the lower registers.

ee. Sing the exercise to fixed pitches. "Sneeze" the vowel high in the head and allow it to glide downwards. Spread·the nostrils to amplify the focus for darker vowels: 'u' [u], 'a' [a], 'o' [o]. To encourage better placement in the lower range, lift the upper lips exposing the front teeth:

Ha —tschi
[a] [i]

3. aa. Leaps and falling lines present special vocal problems. It is useful to think in contrary motion to the melodic pattern. (That is, think upward during a descending line and downward for ascending phrases). To demonstrate this sensation, ask the singers to bend at the knees when singing high pitches. For low notes, the choir can stand on tiptoe. Hand motions are added to reinforce the shifts of direction. If the choir masters this concept, the low register will float and the high notes will be warm and round:

u_____(u)_____
[u]
ü_____(ü)
[y]

bb. Further exercises for consistent registers (light, piano and legato singing, low larynx): To save time as well as to allow for proper production of the sound, begin with a simple phrase in quarter note values. Image: Sing through the "chimney" of the head. Maintain this heightened feeling for exercises in chest voice. Allow the low notes to crescendo. Use the opposite sensation for singing the higher exercises:

cc.

4. More imagery: When singing from the upper range into the lower one, imagine that the body expands as if it were bell-shaped. At the same time, the tone must become more slender—never more heavy (once again, a contrary image). Legato: initiate a new vowel sound for each pitch of the phrase to maintain the intensity of the tone and the continuity of the line:

5. Sighing: Begin a sigh as high as possible and continue downward. Use the vowel 'u' [u] as the initial vowel.

II. EXERCISES FOR SPECIFIC TECHNIQUES

All vocalises should begin at a comfortable range and then proceed up or down, depending upon the voices. The conductor can instruct certain sections of the choir to drop out of the exercise when the extremes of the scale are sung. Later on, the singers will know their own abilities well enough to manage alone.

a. Staccato

(Closure, intensity of tone, clear intonation, head voice. exercises for upper register):

1. Pant like a dog. The hands may test the diaphragmatic action around the waist.

2. Transfer the panting to pitches:

'h' [h], 'f' [f], 'h', 'f', and 'h', 'f', 'tsh' [t ʃ], 'h', 'f', 'tsh.'

3. Bark in the lower register like a big dog. Use the vowel 'u' [u]. Squeal in the upper register like a puppy, also on 'u' [u].

4. Bark with 'u' [u], 'o' [o], 'a' [a]. Use the hands to encourage diaphragmatic action. They act as a guard for the singers, directing attention from the throat to the middle of the body. The conductor must convince the choir of the importance of a flexible diaphragm before proceeding to the next step of this exercise. Check a few of the singers to be sure that the abdominal muscles are involved. Otherwise, the singers will produce the staccato notes from the glottis instead of the diaphragm, or by articulating an aspirate [h] before each pitch. Both of these methods are dangerous to good singing. If, however, this foundation is laid properly, staccato singing will be achieved easily.

5. Combine panting and barking with 'h' [h], 'f' [f], 'u' [u]

6. h h h u u u [u]

7. Then try speaking an open vowel supported by a diaphragm push:

o [o]-o-o, u [u]-u-u, a [a]-a-a

8. aa. The same pattern sung:

bb.

9. aa. Check the tempo. Before accelerating the tempo, be sure that each choir member is singing on the breath with a relaxed jaw. As the tempo increases, the diaphragm pushes will be lighter. (Cramping occurs if the pressures are too severe):

bb.

10. To make music from the exercises, one can use a children's song, abstract the text and sing the melody with staccato articulation. Begin slowly and increase the tempo:

Clap, clap, clap your hands, Trad.

11. aa. Remember: The jaw must be kept relaxed. Create exercises with chromatic patterns. Begin with the vowel 'u' [u] and follow with other vowels. Select 'a' [a] for the highest passages. Once the staccato technique has been mastered, offer the singers more difficult intervals:

bb.

cc.

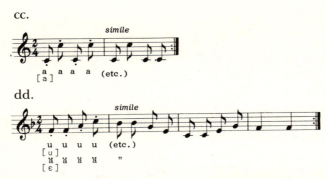

[a] a a a (etc.)

dd.

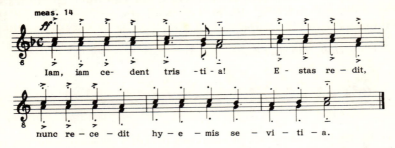

u u u u (etc.)
[u]
ä ä ä ä   "
[ɛ]

12. aa. Staccato singing is very useful for teaching a work. The following example demonstrates this point. This excerpt is conceived to be performed staccato throughout.

"Ecce Gratum" from *Carmina Burana,* Carl Orff

Iam, iam ce- dent tris -ti - a!   E - stas re — dit,

nunc re – ce – dit   hy – e – mis se – vi – ti – a.

bb. But, legato singing can also be taught with staccato technique:

Ave Verum Corpus, Wolfgang Amadeus Mozart

etc.

If the choir sounds tired, breathy, unrhythmic and does not sing precisely together, singers should sing their parts on a neutral 'du' [d u] syllable in staccato, disregarding the rhythmic values. The 'd' activates the diaphragm but can be eliminated by the repetition. For the third repetition, the vowels of the text should be interpolated. Allow time between the syllables so that the next vowel, tone and characteristic sound can be imagined. Now the movement can be sung "legato" with the complete text. Insist that the choir sustain the vowel sounds and speak the consonants crisply.

du   du   du   (etc.)
[u]
[u] u   u   "
[u]
a   ä   ä   a   a   ä   ä   ä   u   u   o   o   u   etc.
[a] [ɛ]   [u]   [o]

b. Development of the high voice

(Expanding the range, securing the consistency of attack and register).

1. Staccato singing is especially useful for training the high voice because it relies on the spontaneous reaction of the vocal mechanism. The singer produces the higher pitches without being aware of a means or method. Thus the common "fear of heights" is relieved. The throat is relaxed and open when the vowel 'u' is sung in brisk mezzo-piano patterns; think the opposite direction:

u   u   u   (etc.)
[u]
ü   ü   ü   "
[y]

In order that the sequence of exercises proceed consecutively, the conductor sings rhythmically the beginning tone between each exercise:

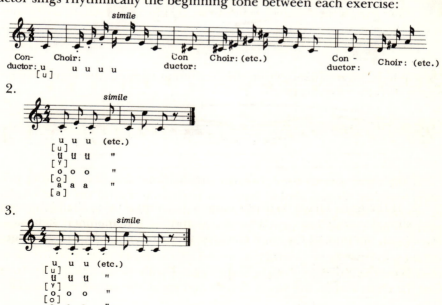

Con-   Choir: Con   Choir: (etc.)   Con -   Choir: (etc.)
ductor: u   u   u   u   u   ductor: ductor:
[u]

2.

u   u   u   (etc.)
[u]
ü   ü   ü   "
[y]
o   o   o   "
[o]
a   a   a   "
[a]

3.

u   u   u   (etc.)
[u]
ü   ü   ü   "
[y]
o   o   o   "
[o]
a   a   a   "
[a]

4. To work against the fear-principle: "that is too high," ask the singer to make an inviting gesture to the side or to the front or to bend slightly at the knees, as if the floor had given way:

5.

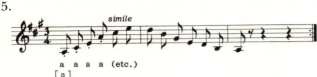

6.

7. Once these exercises have been sung in staccato, they should be repeated in a connected legato line. Choose vocalises which pass through the higher range. Use the vowel 'u' [u] to establish head resonance without producing a thick or forced tone when you go higher. For the descending passages, sing the vowel 'o' [o] with the space for 'a' [a] in the vocal tract:

8. Glide in mezzo-piano; from the beginning imagine the highest pitch. Match the other sounds to it:

9. If the tenors have difficulty with 'u' [u] and 'a' [a] in the high range, they should modify the vowels to 'ue' [y] and 'i' [i]. Remember: Relaxation of the jaw, opening of the vocal tract, slender singing in the upper range:

10.

11.

12.

13. Combine staccato and legato:

It is helpful to follow the staccato exercises (b1-12 above) with identical passages in a sustained style without taking a breath. Unconsciously, the singer will use the diaphragm actively for the staccato version and passively for the legato singing:

c. Legato and cantabile

(Easy flow, connection of syllables, homogenous sound).

Legato means connected; it is indicated by a curved line. This marking for a stringed instrument denotes a manner of performance, that is, all the notes of the particular phrase will be played on one bow. The same principle applies to brass music; the tones under the legato marking are played without separate tongue articulation. In singing, legato and legato phrasing are demonstrated in the strictest sense when several tones are sung on a single syllable (Vocalise). One applies the term "legato" to a series of disjunct tones using various syllables if the syllables are placed closely together. Sustained singing of this type is referred to as "cantabile." In this text "legato" will imply a connected musical phrase, but when this technique is associated with singing, the term "cantabile" defines a specific usage. For the purposes of this book, a phrase marking depicts syllabification—not musical phrasing.

Good legato singing presents a problem for every choir, many bad habits destroy a chain of vowels: poorly articulated consonants (too thick, too long, improperly pronounced), disparate vowel colorings, shallow neutral syllables, insufficient tension for long tones. Each vowel should be guided to the next one. If this procession of sounds does not occur, suggest to the choir that the succeeding sound must begin while the preceding tone is sounding.

1. A prerequisite for good legato singing is a steady, flexible breath support (See B I,d,1-3) and a thorough understanding of register adjustments aided by vowel modifications. (See B II,d-ff) Prepare with a sigh; allow the air to fall into the body, (astonishment) (See A II,c,4). Wait a few seconds before allowing the breath to stream out of the lungs on 's'. This sound is emitted uniformly—no stuttering or quivering. Image: the breath is a laser-beam traveling through the wall. Follow its path with a pointing finger. The breast bone remains high so that the position of the rib cage does not change even when the abdomen retracts. Repeat the sigh. This time exhale on the consonant combination 'sh' [ʃ]—sigh again. (Sighing relieves any strain on the heart which may be created by extended breath exercises).

2. Sing the vowel 'u' [u] on a sustained flow of air in piano dynamic:

3. Maintain an even tone quality; do not increase in volume, rather sing to a goal (laser-beam). Choose a pitch level in the middle range of the voice where head quality is audible. Thus the voice can glide more easily for the following exercises:

4. In piano dynamic. Image: Each tone longs to reach the next tone. Keep the voice steady:

5. Transpose the exercise chromatically up and down. Image: Think the vowel 'u' [u] while singing the vowel 'o' [o] (vowel modification), (See B II,d). Rounded mouth position (fishmouth):

6. Shape the mouth for the vowel before inhaling; breathe through the vowel. "See, hear and feel" the vowel prior to singing. Always attack gently with no breath pressure or glottal stroke. A thread of sound spins itself through a firm support:

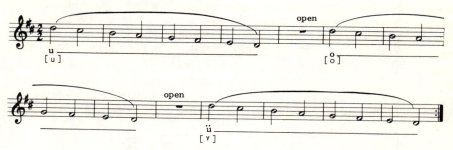

7. Avoid sliding by reiterating the vowel sound for each tone. Open the mouth in a "fishmouth" form as if for the vowel 'o' [o] but slightly more open:

8. Preserve the rounded mouth position of 'u' [u] and 'o' [o] for the bright vowels 'i' [i] and 'ä' [ɛ]. Add a smile, exposing the upper teeth. Do not spread the mouth horizontally:

48

9. For open 'a' [a] or 'o' [ɔ], imagine the 'u' [u] vowel opens the throat:

10.

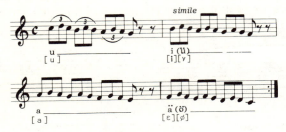

11. Then sing on all other vowels:

12. Sing on all vowels:

13.

14. Consonants will be slipped between the vowels. Begin with the voiced fricative and nasal consonants. When properly produced, these consonants carry with them a neutral vowel sound (ə—schwa). Allow the consonants to sound.

[ŋ] [m] [n] [l] [v] [z]:

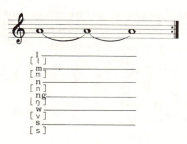

15. 'L' [l] resonates highest in the mask resonance when it is formed by the tip of the tongue resting lightly on the alveolar ridge. Amateur singers may wish to practice by extending and retracting the tongue over the upper lip. The consonant 'l' [l] receives the same rhythmic value as the 'u' [u]. This applies to exercises 16, 17, and 18 also:

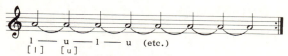

l — u — l — u (etc.)
[l]   [u]

16. Sing the 'l' [l] with the mouth in the 'u' [ú] position; there should be no break between the consonant and the vowel. Imagine that phonation occurs from a "third eye," which resides at the bridge of the nose:

l — u — l — u (etc.)
[l] [u]
v — u — v — u   "
[v]
z — u — z — u   "
[z]

17. The tongue touches the hard palate at the alveolar ridge to make the consonant 'n' [n]. The consonant 'm' [m] requires maximum space in the mouth achieved with a loose jaw. Again, the vowel 'u' [u] is used at the outset because of the low laryngeal position it supplies. Often sustained consonants are formed by constricting the mouth space. Remember this danger when the exercises are sung to other vowels:

n — u — n — u   (etc.)
m — u — m — u   "
[u]

18. The nasal consonant combination 'ng' [ŋ] brings into play the jaw hanging by its own weight. Use other vowels:

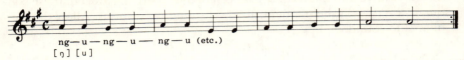

ng—u—ng—u—ng—u (etc.)
[ŋ] [u]

19. aa. When performing these melodies, prolong the consonants longer than usual. In legato singing, the consonant seizes its time from the note value preceding the vowel, so that it would be written:

lu vu su mu nu ngu lu
[l][u][v] [z]   [ŋ]

bb.

lu___v u___s u___m u___n u___ng u___l u
[u]   [z]   [ŋ]

20.

lo   vo   so   mo   no   ngo   lo   vo
[o] [v] [z]   [ŋ]
la   va   sa   ma   na   nga   la   va
[a] [v] [z]   [ŋ]
le   ve   se   me   ne   nge   le   ve
[e]

21.

li___   va—— ma—— na——
[j]
lu___   va—— ma—— na——
[y]
le___   va—— ma—— na——
[e]

22. Once the choir has been trained to place the consonants precisely and quickly, advance to long vowels and short consonants in a resonate stream of sound. Select a familiar tune and vary the vowels:

Lullaby, Johannes Brahms

mu mu mi   mu mu   mi   mu mu mi   mi   mu mi   mi   ma ma   mi   mi   ma ma
[u]   [i]   [a]

mi   ma ma   mi mi ma   ma   mi   mu mu mi   mu mu   mi   mu mu

mi mi mi   mu   mu mu mu mo   mu mu mo   mu mu mo   mo   mu   mu
[o]

Transpose the melody upwards chromatically. Encourage consistency in the vocal registers by vowel modification (See B II,d,1-4). 'u' [u], 'o' [o], 'a' [a] for the higher register, 'i' and 'e' for the lower register, or use the umlauts 'ü' [y] and 'ö' [∅]. Observe carefully each vowel sound. Each vowel receives the same intensity. The open 'a' possesses a tendency to be flaccid. Vary the consonants, but sustain the vowels for equal duration.

The so-called explosive consonants pose special problems for legato singing. It is a common observation that the German language is not conducive to singing because of its excessive use of consonants. The language acquires its character through bundles of consonants. For this reason, the treatment of consonants requires careful attention. The pattern of the consonants creates the skeleton of the German language. Textual pictures are created by these patterns, enhancing the expressive quality of the language. In combination with some corresponding vowel sounds, the consonants colorfully illustrate the content of the text. The profusion attracts the listener's interest. In terms of vocal technique, the articulation of consonants involves an active diaphragm which "shoots" the vowels to their proper placement.

The faster the singer can speak the consonants on a flexible current of air, the thicker will be the flow of the legato line. The tongue, lips, jaw, and soft palate are involved in this transaction (Exercises for their activation: See B I,g-i). Here are the consonants to be practiced:

'f' [f], 'v' [v], 'sh' [ʃ], 'ch' [tʃ], 'b' [b], 'p' [p], 'd' [d], 't' [t], 'g' [g], 'k' [k].

Remember: each consonant dwells in its own particular location along the vocal tract depending upon the vowel it precedes. Test the position of the tongue in the formation of the following syllables:

ku [u], ko [o], ka [a], kä [ɛ], ki [i]   pu, po, pa, pä, pi
bu, bo, ba, bä, bi   gu, go, ga, gä, gi

23. The singer must be aware of this modulation. During the rests in the following exercise, imagine the next vowel in the sequence. Automatically, the consonant will be shaped in relation to the vowel. One avoids unnecessary muscle tension and eliminates one complete step. The throat must be open for this process (using the vowel 'u' [u] as an ideal):

24. A series of different vowels in a legato phrase without rests: one hears the second vowel while the first vowel is sounding (See 23 above). Image: The vowels travel on a conveyor belt, on an escalator, or in an elevator (the vocal tract) without interruption from one vowel to another. The consonants are not driven with the vowels but rather act indepen-

dently from the front of the mouth:

25.

26. aa. Application of legato exercises to a familiar song with sustained character. The song should be written on the blackboard to be sung on the syllable "nu" [n u]. Be certain that the vowels do not loose intensity. Energy is especially difficult to perpetuate when intervallic skips occur. Commonly a crescendo happens during upward leaps. Avoid any variance of dynamics.

The singer must learn the shape of the phrase as well as the method of connecting the vowel sounds. In order to guide the melody to its climax, the conductor may designate the most important pitch or word. Warning: Keep the end of the line in the mind's eye and ear from the first tone to be sung:

Rock a Bye Baby, Traditional

cc. Sing the vowels of the song in succession:

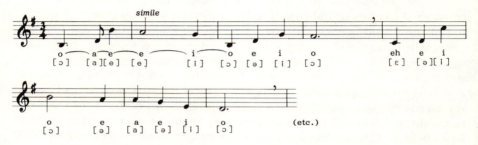

dd. Sing the vowel chain with a 'd' [d] before each note:

ee. Here the text is noted as the choir should sing it; the vowels will be divided by rests of equal value to provide the choir time to prepare the bundles of consonants to be articulated between the beats. The concept of legato singing should be clear:

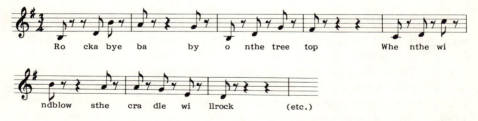

From exercise ee, it is obvious that only the main vowel of a diphthong is sung ('ei' = an 'a' is sung, an 'i' is intimated).

ff. Now sing the melody with its proper text. The results of exercise c,26,ee above should be audible:

Ro - cka-bye ba - by o - nthe tree - top. Whe -nthe wi -

ndblows the cra - dle wi - llrock. (etc.)

27. aa. In addition to the above-mentioned legato singing, one must consider the colors of the vowels to be unified in a choral sound. A blending of the sound is necessary for a true legato line. Prefixes and suffixes with the neutral vowel [ə] (er, en, em, et, ed, es, el, ge, te, je, he, ke, le, me, ne, pe, re, se, ve, we) are spoken and sung without emphasis. Amateur singers tend to open these syllables to a shallow 'eh' [ɛ]. A help: Form a rounded mouth opening encouraging a vowel coloration of 'ö' [œ] (as in the German word "moechte"). A similar process can be used for the prefixes: (herein, herauf, herunter, gegeben; or desire, retrieve, receive, relieve, believe, repeat). Neutral prefixes are more closed syllables than neutral suffixes. The vowel 'ue' [y] may assist dark, unaccented end syllables (müssen, kitchen, for example):

Rock - a - bye ba - by on the tree - top,
[ə] [ə] [ə]

blows the cra - dle will rock, when the bough breaks the
[ə] [ə] [ə] [ə]

cra - dle will fall and down will come ba - by cra - dle and all.
[ə] [ə]

bb. The short 'u' [ʊ] (dunkel, Nuss, Nummer, muss, foot, put, soot, full); 'i' [ɪ] (immer, in, Stimme, Sinne, symbol, dinner, minute, signal, in); 'o' [ɔ] (wollen, sollen, rollen, voll, troll, roll, toll); 'e' [ɛ] (messen, essen, rennen, Welle, medical, ethical, reminiscent, Wellington) have primarily an unmixed chest quality. To match these vowels with those in higher registers, one modifies the short vowels to long vowels. (This concept is particularly advantageous for the female voice but can be helpful to the male voice also):

For example the word "foot":

From a (A) through a' (a) .... sing open = "soot" [ʊ]
From a' (a) through d'' (d') ... sing somewhat more closed = "soon" [u]
From d'' (d') through g'' (g') ... sing a long closed sound, as if you add some vowels = "moooooon" [u]

The vowels 'i' [ɪ], 'uh' [ʌ], 'o' [ɔ] should be treated like 'u':

Sing for 'i' in "sit" [ɪ]:
      1. open = "him" [ɪ]
      2. more closed = "see" [i]
      3. long closed = "freeeeze" [i]

Sing for 'uh' in "must" [ʌ]:
      1. open = "dust" [ʌ]
      2. more closed = "father" [a]
      3. long closed = "gaaaaarden" [a]

Sing for 'o' in "morning" [ɔ]
      1. open = "boring" [ɔ]
      2. more closed = "so" [o] (no diphthong!)
      3. long closed = "choooosen" [o] (no diphthong!)

Treat the ae [ɛ] as follows:

From a (A) through a' (a) .... sing open = "better" [ɛ]
From a' (A) through d'' (d') .... sing somewhat more closed = "sad" [ɛ]
From d'' (d') through g'' (g') .... the vocal tract is open as if for ae but the vowel coloration emphasizes the quality of a closed e [e]. A mixture of the vowel i [i] is implied.

RESULT: The vowel sound is heard at all times. The consonant becomes a grace note configuration to each vowel. The listener discerns a constant stream of resonance.

d. Vowel modification

(Consistency of registers; expressive singing through vowel color changes, echo, crescendo, decrescendo).

The human voice consists in three natural regions: head, middle and chest registers. The tone which is ideal for artistic expression unites the best qualities of all three registers. The main goal of vocal technique is to disguise the adjustments between registers clearly. The voice will sound as if it had only one register. Since each vowel has its own resonating area, the vowels become useful for the alignment of the voice.

Suppose one sings the vowel 'a' [a] which opens the vocal tract. If the vowel sounds shallow and needs more focus, one can imagine the forward position of the vowel 'i' [i]. The vocal tract shapes itself differently conforming to the 'i' [i] configuration. (See also B II c,26.bb).

The conductor should be able to evaluate the choral sound the choir produces in terms of the vowel colors. The shades which vowels possess can be painted like the hues of a painter's palette.

1. aa. For instance, if the choir sings the following passage with thin, pressed tones, which seem to be swallowed:

na   na   na   (etc.)
[a]

Ask the group to reduce the size of the mouth opening. With each successive pitch, the mouth space will be increased as the jaw drops:

na   na   na   (etc.)
[a]

bb. Higher pitches require more space in the vocal tract and in the mouth. Think the vowel 'u' [u] to open the throat and focus the sound. Sing the exercise on 'u' [u] and then on 'a' [a]. Rest both hands on the cheeks to direct the movement of the jaw (the jaw falls down and backwards, it should not be shoved forward):

nu   nu   nu   (etc.)
[u]
na   na   na   na(nu)na   na   na
[a]

2. aa. Inherently the vowel 'i' [i] sounds tight and pinched; so sing the exercise first on 'fra.'

bb. Next, sing the phrase on 'ü' [y] with the mouth open as if an 'a' [a] were being sung.

cc. Then sing the phrase on 'free,' think 'ü' [y], each time dropping the jaw for the large skips:

free _____

dd. Follow with a version of the exercise on 'nä' [ɛ] whereby the singer imagines the forward placement of the 'i' [i] vowel. For extremely high ranges of the voice, one should sing the vowels indicated using the mouth opening for the vowel 'a' [a]. When the melody descends to a more comfortable range, the given vowels should be sung:

(8)   He _____ leaves _____ me
(Ha   laves   ma)
[a]   [a]   [a]

3. Often difficulties arise from the vowel 'ä' [ɛ], because of its dialectic variations in speech. The amateur singer stretches the lips horizontally and presses the sound into the throat. To counteract:

aa. The choir sings the following exercise on 'na' [a] with a singer's fishmouth, the jaw falls open with each intervallic leap to reinforce the feeling of relaxation during phonation.

bb. Next sing the phrase on 'noe' [ø] with the mouth open as if an 'a' [a] were being sung. The sound will be brighter and more transparent.

cc. Then sing the phrase on 'ni' [i] each time dropping the jaw for the larger skips. 'i' [i] is a key vowel for tonal focus.

dd. Follow with a version of the exercise on 'nae' [ɛ] whereby the singer imagines the forward placement of the 'i' [i] vowel.

ee. Sing the passage with text. The jaw should react instinctively to the wide leaps. Each will be modified to 'i' [i] in the upper register.

The conductor's ear notes the degree of warmth or point needed for proper assimilation of the 'ä' [ɛ] to the textual phrase. The basic premise remains: a balance between the space for 'a' and the focus of 'i' [i] (See B II, c,26,bb.):

Oh yes___ he has ___ the shells___ to share.

4. The concept of a brighter vowel coloration will change thick, chest tones to slender, cohesive sounds. Consider a melodic line with open 'a' [a] vowels dominating the text:

My moth - er likes the sun so much.

aa. Sing the phrase on 'li' through rounded lips, the upper teeth exposed; the 'l' [l] sets up the frontal placement of the 'i' [i]:

li li li (etc.)
[i]

bb. Add the vowel 'a' [a] to the syllable but do not alter the mouth position. The tongue should not be disturbed:

li- a li - a li - a (etc.)
[i][a]

cc. Sing the phrase on 'la' [a] while thinking the sensation of the 'i' [i] vowel. The lips and teeth used for the 'i' [i] sound will keep the sound from slipping back into the throat.

dd. Now sing the passage with the text, applying this method to the open 'a' [ə] vowels.

5. If the lower voices (alto and bass) are to sing wide leaps into the chest register, they may be tempted to drop the tones into their throats, procuring a brutal and hollow sound. Systematic vowel modification counterbalances the tendency by emphasizing a higher point of focus:

        Bar -   ba - ra

aa. Sigh on the vowel 'a' [ə] several times from the upper register through the lower.

bb. Sigh as in aa. and attempt to arrive on a particular pitch indicated by the conductor (g' for example). Move from an open mouth to a partially closed one.

cc. Begin again in the upper range. Sing a glissando from one fixed pitch to another. The mouth opening will coincide with the pitch level as above. Preserve the sensation of sighing while singing this example:

    a   (ŏ)   a   (ŏ)   a   (ŏ)   a   (ŏ)

dd. The exercise can be sung with a text using the results of 5 cc.:

Bar - ba - ra   (etc.)
[ə]
      (bo - ro)
      [ɔ]

6. aa. Vowel modification serves the singer for expressive purposes also. Suppose, for instance, the musical structure of a work exhibits an echo effect. The conductor can ask that the passage be sung in a softer dynamic with a smaller mouth opening. This is an easy way to reach one's goal. An attentive listener will notice how the intensity of the forte 'a' [a], for example, becomes an open but piano 'o' [ɔ]. The average audience recognizes only how the tone remains constant. By decreasing the space in the mouth, the tone can be held in the mask resonance even during sudden dynamic shifts. In a similar manner, the following vowels migrate:

o————u,   i————ü,   ä————ö

[o]   [u]   [i]   [y]   [ɛ]   [œ]

bb.

our	fa	-	ther,	our	fa -	ther
see	me	lea	-	ving,	see me lea -	ving
bet	-ter	fat	-	ter,	bet-ter fat -	ter
go	to - mor	-	row,	go	to -mor -	row

7. Vowel migration can affect a crescendo or decrescendo. Begin by singing the vowel 'u' [u] in a limited space. Gradually free the vowel by opening the mouth. The result will be a chain of vowels from 'o' [o] to 'o' [ɔ] to 'a' [a]:

8. The reverse creates a decrescendo. Decrease the space very slowly, noting the many gradations of vowel adjustments from forte to pianissimo. Most amateur choral groups perform decrescendi too hastily allowing the tonal intensity to wane:

9. For long, sustained pitches, a certain vitality can be captured by adjusting the vowel sounds. Open the vowel progressively to give the singer a goal toward which to sing (do not make a crescendo):

e. Martellato

(Coloratura in Baroque literature, word-painting).

It is especially difficult to teach martellato technique to a group of singers. Time, patience and eagerness are essential. Without individual assistance, very few members of a choir will be able to master this particular skill artfully.

1. As part of its heritage, choral music belongs to the Baroque era with its long melismatic passages and rhythmic flourishes. Example:

60

2. The conductor should not grab for inadequate short cuts (described in 2aa). like dividing the rapid notes of a florid passage with aspirate 'h's, or smearing the tones of sixteenth-note chains, or (as in 2bb.) adding a consonant before the vowel:

Der Geist hilft unsrer Schwachheit Auf, J. S. Bach

aa.

Der   Gei ha ha ha ha ha   (etc.)
[e]   [a]

bb.

Der   Gei da da da da da   (etc.)
[e]   [a]

3. The word "martellato" means "hammered" (martellato = the hammer, in Italian) and describes a legato line with flexible accentuation. Each tone receives a brisk pressure from the diaphragm. In effect, the legato line becomes a series of momentary crescendi and decrescendi:

a
[a]

Use the staccato exercises in B II,a,1-12 as a foundation.

4. Follow with exercises which combine legato and staccato to prepare the diaphragm for the development of martellato techniques:

o   o   o   (etc.)
[o]   staccato   legato

5.

a   a   a   (etc.)
[a]

6.

u   u   u   u   (etc.)
[u]

7. The following exercise illustrates the basic concept of the phrase as defined by a legato marking. The staccato points the bouncing motion of diaphragmatic pressures:

8. So that these indications are not mistaken as 'portato' marks, martellato will be noted by a tenuto mark over a staccato point. (Diaphragm pressure held the length of the note value.):

Sing the following exercises at such a tempo that every tone can be controlled by the diaphragm. Do not be lured into the habit of articulating the pitches with an aspirate 'h' or a glottal attack:

9.

10.

11.

12. If coloratura is to be sung at a fast tempo, as is usually the case, it would seem logical to seek a compromise for inexperienced singers. Jaw movements have been used throughout this text for various purposes (See B I,f,1-3 and B I,k,2,aa.-cc.). For coloratura singing, the jaw can serve to divide the tones of a vocalise. The effect of martellato will be achieved if one accents with a diaphragm impulse the first note of a rhythmic group. The other notes of the group will be separated by an easy motion of the jaw.

In exercises 12,aa.-cc. jaw flexibility is encountered again. The chin moves as if it were engaged in chewing (with an open mouth). Use a hand to be sure that the movements occur. Amateur singers tend to be victims of tense and cramped facial parts. Many will attempt this exercise with a closed mouth. Yawning between the exercises will relax the face and throat.

Always begin slowly; each repetition can be faster. As the tempo accelerates, the jaw movements should be smaller. For a melisma marked vivace, the jaw simply trembles. Observe jaw exercises in a mirror:

aa.

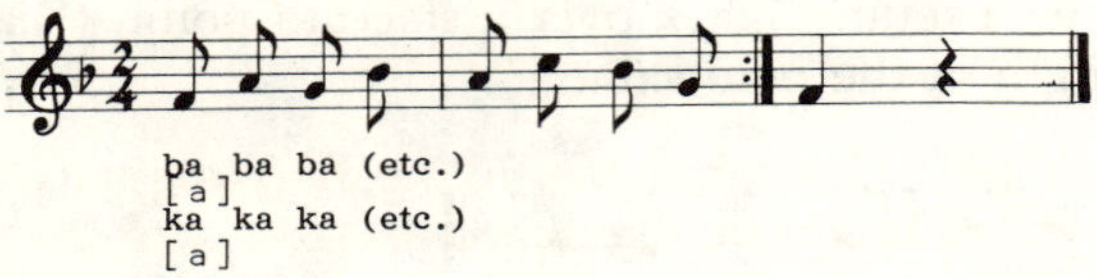

ba ba ba (etc.)
[a]
ka ka ka (etc.)
[a]

bb.

na na na (etc.)
[a]
da da da (etc.)
[a]

cc.

da da da (etc.)
[a]

13. The next exercises (13,aa,bb,cc) are based upon the material learned in exercises 12,aa,bb,cc. An impulse from the diaphragm is added to each jaw motion (See B II,1ff). Both the diaphragmatic pressure and its accompanying jaw action should remain brief and flexible. Introduce this concept with a series of sharp consonants.

When the attention is drawn to the diaphragm, do not neglect the jaw. The conductor must watch and correct each singer. The singer's face may appear strained and unnatural at first. Perhaps the jaw movement is being exaggerated. It should be playful in character in order to produce the desired musical result:

aa.

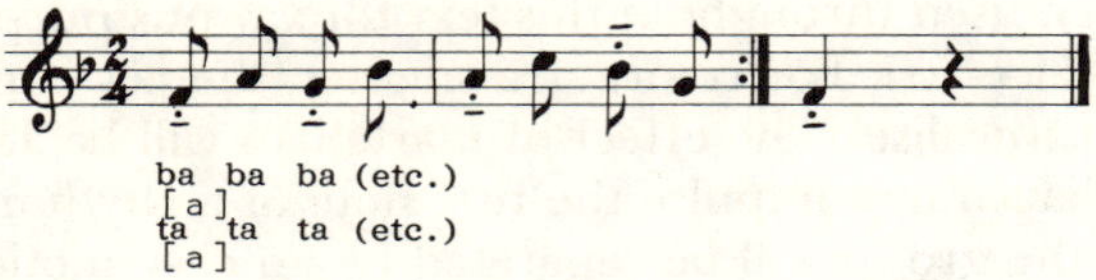

ba ba ba (etc.)
[a]
ta ta ta (etc.)
[a]

bb.

ta ta ta (etc.)
[a]

cc.

ta ta ta (etc.)
[a]

14. The next exercises (14,aa,bb,cc) retain the diaphragmatic pressures of earlier exercises (13,aa,bb,cc) on the notes marked with the following sign (⌄). For exercise 14 aa. the first two notes on beat 1 have a consonant preceding the vowel in both measures. The third and fourth notes (both on beat 2) have only one consonant between them. The consonant receives a diaphragm pressure and the open vowel gains its identity from the jaw. Here the separation desired comes from the jaw motion as if one pronounced a consonant to acquire the martellato effect. Proceed with exercises 14 bb, cc in similar manner:

aa.

ba ba ba⎯ ba ba ba⎯ ba
[a]

bb.

da da da (etc.)
[a]

cc.

da da da da⎯ da da da da⎯ (etc.)
[a]

15. The final exercises (15,aa,bb,cc) abandon the crutch of helper consonants. The main tones of the line are given an impulse from the diaphragm. The other tones rely on a jaw movement for clarity. Herewith is the martellato technique complete:

64

aa.

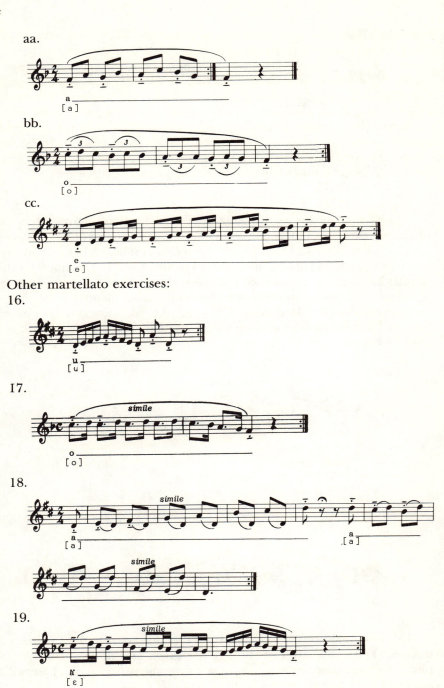

bb.

cc.

Other martellato exercises:
16.

17.

18.

19.

Decide upon the manner of martellato singing by the tempo of the music. At a moderato gait, all the singers could articulate each note with a diaphragm pressure. For more florid singing, the combination of dia-phragm and jaw motions interchangeably will be more efficient.

20. Martellato lines should never be performed at a stagnant dynamic. The following, typical flourish gains clarity and interest when it is sung with a slight rise and fall in volume. If one relaxes the dynamic near the end of the dotted note, the diaphragm will relax sufficiently to grip the succeeding sixteenth notes for better definition. Do not interrupt the stream of tone for the line will become "bumpy." When singing the exercise faster, divide the activity between the diaphragm and the jaw:

21.

22. Practice different types of martellato figures in long thematic phrases. Transpose the passages freely:

23.

24.

25.

26.

27. aa. Combine alternately scales in martellato and legato to improve technical skill and satisfy expressive needs in musical contexts:

bb.

cc.

28.

29. Martellato can give emphasis to specific textual elements. The diaphragm underscores a word of the text:

The Last Words of David, Randall Thompson

Sop: rul-ing in the fear of God, ruling in the fear of

God, the fear of God. (etc.)

30.

Cantate Domino, Heinrich Schütz

31. In many works of the Renaissance and Baroque, a tone will be repeated immediately on a single syllable as a form of ornamentation or word painting. In order not to destroy the flow of sound, as staccato technique implies, set the note apart by articulating a new vowel sound with the jaw:

Mass for five voices, "Benedictus," William Byrd

32.

De profundis, Josquin Desprez

33.

Ne irascaris, William Byrd

Chapter C

Warm-Up Exercises based on Chapters A and B, designed to develop various choral sounds indicative of musical style periods and to confront specific problems of individual compositions.

I. WARM-UP SESSIONS BEFORE REHEARSALS

The instruments of each epoch of music history had different shapes and sounds. (Refer to museum catalogues and encyclopedia descriptions.) Musical results correspond to the instruments upon which the works were played. One defines a "sound ideal" for each compositional period. One assumes that vocal works were influenced by these concepts also. Music of Mozart (Classic) does not resemble the music of Wagner (new German-late Romantic-culmination). Nor is Bach's style (late Baroque) like that of Max Reger (late Romantic). Thus a specific vocal interpretation must be designed for choral voice training to bespeak these style periods. The vocalises will form the scaffolding upon which the music is hung. When this dimension of music-making has been explored, the works of composers contemporary to any period of music can be recognized from their individual characteristics (Ex: Bach/Handel, David/Distler). Furthermore, significant differences can be made between the identifying motives of works by the same composers (Ex: Schütz, *Musikalische Exequien* versus *Psalmen Davids*).

"The human voice is capable of greater diversity of tone quality than man-made musical instruments. The vocal tract is sensitive to a variety of sounds as a changing instrument throughout the course of musical history. It is possible to compare the types of trumpets constructed during the early Egyptian times with a contemporary example. This comparison would yield gradations indigenous to the development of this musical source. The singer adjusts subtly the shape of the vocal tract by dilating the pharyngeal region, by modifying vowels to encourage head or chest voice or nasal resonance, by increasing the vibrato or by imagining a darker, warmer, brighter or cooler sound. In addition to these functions, articulation, dynamics and timbre serve to broaden the scope of vocal treatment." (Ehmann, Wilhelm, *Voce et Tuba,* pg. 452, Bärenreiter, Kassel, 1976).

Six illustrations for warm-ups follow. It is assumed that the choral group has grown accustomed to the concept of choral voice building. The fundamental skills described in previous chapters are considered the preparatory steps. Isolated exercises are excerpted and combined with others to address a particular vocal problem or musical circumstance.

The exercises should be repeated in several keys (tonalities). The conductor may wish to improvise other melodic passages to approximate the choir's need more precisely.

a. **General**	d. **Classic**
b. **Renaissance**	e. **Romantic**
c. **Baroque**	f. **Modern (Avant-garde)**

a. General

Objective: To relax the body, especially the vocal tract (pharyngeal and laryngeal regions, resonating cavities) and to prepare for vowel and consonant formants, coloratura, high and low registers.

1. Relaxation of the body. While standing, stretch the arms above the head pulling the body upwards. Bend to touch the floor with the fingertips. Roll the head to either side. At the same time, flex the knees and roll the shoulders. Shake the feet and legs, arms and hands (See A I,a and b, and B I,a,1-5).

2. aa. Begin with exhalation. Exhalation eases body tension. It sets forth the concept of allowing the air to fall into the body. (Try to avoid using the word "inhale" during relaxation sessions.)

Sigh on 'u' [u]. Pant like a dog. Intense diaphragm impulses. (Keep chest high as the air escapes). Inhalation exercises should follow, using consonants pertaining to the text to be sung. This practice encourages precise articulation of the consonants (See B I,c,1 and 2). A hand on the abdomen will guide the diaphragm's activity:

f, f, f,	p, t, p, t, p, t
p, t, k, p, t, k	f, s, sh, f, s, sh

bb.

f f f f (etc.)

s sss s s sh   sh   f f   f f

3. Insert breath "suspension." Suspension implies a slight anticipation of inhalation causing a hunger for air (See B I,e,1-5).

4. Wail like a siren with 'm' [m], 'v' [v], 's' [s], or rolled 'r' [r]. (See A III,c,3.)

5. Sing the melodic pattern of the exercise on the consonant 'v' [v] with a descending sigh as a preparation:

6. To relax the jaw, use the vowels in a series, preceding each sound with an explosive consonant. (See B I,f,3.) Open vowels, like 'a' [a] will not "slip into the throat" if the attention of the singer is drawn to the falling jaw. The vowel is hardly heard:

7. The drum exercise for complete closure of the vocal folds: gradually direct the choir towards the singing of vowels. Each exercise should begin in a comfortable middle range in combination with sustained consonants like 'm' [m] or 'n' [n]. The drum exercise consists in a sustained 'm' [m] broken by a short 'o' [ɔ]:

8. The drumming pattern is combined with legato passages:

9. As in 7 (above), the pitches are to be sung quickly and playfully. To maintain the heady quality, change the vowel systematically from 'no' [o] to

'ne' [e̞] to 'na' [a]. Be attentive to the mouth position. It should be rounded throughout the exercise:

no no no no (etc.)
[o]
ne ne ne ne   "
[e̞]
na na na na   "
[a]

10. Exhale a steady stream of air on 's.' Interjecting this exercise between other technical drills will remind the singer that the process of phonation must occur "on the breath." (See A II,bb. 7.) Shift from 's' [s] to 'z' [z] in the middle range. The hands are used as guides for the diaphragmatic-intercostal muscles.

11. Sing a descending legato scale passage. Begin with the syllable 'nu' [u] (to open the throat). Check breath support. At higher pitch levels, begin the passage with 'na' [a] widening the vocal tract. Transpose the exercise chromatically up to e-major using the following syllable modification:

'na' [a], 'no' [o], 'nu' [u], na, no, nu, na, no, nu

As the scale is sung, imagine an ascending motion (register consistency). This exercise requires much concentration for proper coordination. Therefore, sigh repeatedly between the exercises (perhaps after alternate repetitions). Select a slow tempo. (See B I,a,5.):

nu   na   nu   na   nu   na   nu   na
[u]   [a]
In higher ranges: (na   no   nu   na   no   nu   na   no)
[a]   [o]   [u]

12. Initiate vowel placement with those consonants which originate in the mask, ('n' [n] and 'j' [j]). Move from the well-placed 'u' [u] of the previous exercise through 'ue' [y] to arrive at 'i' [i]. Use the same method for 'e' [e]. (See B I,j,7,bb and cc.) If the 'nj' [nj] is extended, the vowel can be shoved into its proper placement (forward placement):

catch breath   catch breath   catch breath   catch breath

nju njü nji   njo njö nje   nju njü nji   (etc.)
[u] [y] [i]   [o] [ø] [e]

13. Combine legato and martellato techniques, transposing the patterns as above. (See B II,e,4-6):

ni
[j]
na
[ɛ]

14. Change to a faster tonal series, adding intervallic leaps. Transpose the series upward chromatically. (See B II,b,1,ff.) Modify all the vowels:

```
da   da  (etc.)
[ a ]
di   di     "
[ i ]
dä   dä     "
[ ɛ ]
```

15. Preparation for the low register. In the first part of the exercise, the middle range is emphasized. Thereafter, the line dips into the chest register. Think of the phrase as an ascending passage, so that the tones do not slide down the throat. Transpose the exercise downward chromatically. Add a hand motion to strengthen the contrasting sensation:

```
mi              mi
[ i ]
mä              mä
[ ɛ ]
mo              mo
[ o ]
```

16. Preparation for the high register. Approach the higher voice with staccato. The singers who are not equipped to sing in the upper register should be excused from the transposed exercises as soon as the singing becomes uncomfortable. Sing short, punctuated notes on 'a' [a], keeping the vocal tract open. As the phrase leaps to the octave, flex the knees (See B II,b,1-5.):

```
  o   o   o   o    o   o   o
[ o ]
(a   a   a   a    a   a   a)
[ a ]
```

17. Sing all the vowels on a steady stream over a standing harmony. Raise and lower the pitch level of the chords chromatically. This exercise serves as a drill for ear training also. The crescendo and decrescendo indicated should be executed evenly:

```
nu      no      na      ne      ni
[ u ]   [ o ]   [ a ]   [ e ]   [ i ]
```

b. Renaissance

Sound ideal: between polyphony and homophony, static and forward motion, blended sound, minimal vibrato, legato.

1. Relaxation. Circulation of blood in the region of the vocal mechanism. Stand and stretch the body. Yawn as if it were early morning. Wave with the left arm and then with the right arm. Wave both arms simultaneously. Imitate the movement of a snake. Make the movement to the front, to the sides; include finger motions. Slap the body as if there were dust on it. Beat the chest with both fists. Nod "yes" and "no" with the head. Shift the body weight from the heels to the toes and back. Step in place and sigh on 'u' [u]. (See A I,a-c and B I,a,1-5.)

2. Flexibility of jaw and tongue to release the vocal tract and to guard against an unnatural vibrato: Sit down comfortably. Rest the head on the chest. The jaw hangs down; the tongue reposes on the lower lip. Shake the head energetically, so that the tongue and jaw are jostled. Make a fishmouth. Form circles with the jaw. (The tongue lies flat, as if it were a wet rag.) Move the jaw up and down, back and forth. Extend and retract the tongue rapidly; run the tongue around the teeth, lick the lips. Make the sound of a horse "prhh." Yawn on an 'a' [a]. (See B I,g,h.)

3. To improve breath support, the torso must be held erect. Amateur singers fall into the habit of collapsing the chest as the breath escapes. Supply sufficient breath exercises to insure good posture for the choir while standing and especially while sitting.

Stand up. Take on a singer's posture (See B I,b,1-6 and A I,b). Spread the fingers between the navel and the breastbone. There should be no tension or motion in the shoulders. Think deep into the body. Slowly and intensely release the air on 'ss', wait a few seconds and inhale as if through a straw. The air is "sucked up from the floor" filling the body to the rib cage. Wait a few seconds—exhale on 'f' (the fingers continue to guide the diaphragmatic action). Inhale by slurping the air through two straws. Exhale all the air suddenly on 'tsh' [tʃ]. Increase the number of straws for each repetition. Sigh (See B I,e,1-6).

4. Phonation aided by consonants 'v' [v], 's' [s], 'l' [l]. The sound is led to the mask. Slurp in the air through three straws. Breathe out on a half-spoken/half-sung 'v' [v]. Each singer chooses their own range. A tone cluster occurs. Wait a few seconds—exhale through four straws. Wait. By the same method, expel the air on 'z' [z], then on 'l' [l]. The tone sits between the eyes (in the third eye). (See B I,j,2.)

5. aa. An 'l' [l] prepares the head quality for a legato in piano (high soft singing). Sigh. Imagining great astonishment, let the air fall into the body. Begin the tone without pressure. The 'l' [l] places the tone between the eyes. Sing a descending passage concentrating on forward placement for each tone.

Thinking in the opposite direction will help maintain the connection between the pitch and the resonators. The tip of the tongue lies on the alveolar ridge. Tension at the base of the tongue must be eliminated. The chest cavity remains high and immobile, even during extreme exhalation. The thought of shock or astonishment may help produce the buoyancy in the chest required:

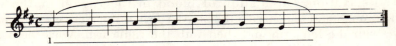

bb. Allow an 'u' [u] to emerge from the 'l' [ɪ]. (See B I,j,3.):

cc. Develop 'o' [o] and 'a' [a] from this basis (low larynx, high resonance). Do not enlarge the mouth opening. Point the upper lip for the 'a' [a]. The singers can "stretch a rubber band" with both hands. The jaw should be relaxed:

6. aa. Add the bright vowels using 'u' [u] as a point of reference. (See 5 cc). Imagine space in the throat. Increase the sound, acquiring more of the resonance of the middle voice. Breathe passively with minimum vibrato. Demonstrate the shape of the phrase with a hand gesture. Hear the beginning of the next phrase while the final tone of the preceding phrase sounds. (See B I,j,4.):

bb.

7. To create the sensation of mixed vowels, divide the voices into groups. Each group is assigned a different vowel. This method can apply to register consistency. (See B II,d.) Pronounce the consonants quickly.

Image: The second note of each pair is slightly longer than the first:

All voices sing (S & T: di —— do —— da —— de —— di
at the same time) [i] [o] [a] [e] [i]
A & B: di —— de —— da —— do —— du
[i] [e] [a] [o] [u]

8. Intervals which are intrinsic to the melody must not interrupt its flow. Sing the legato line without consonants at first. The singer becomes aware of the close relation between the vowels. "Lay the consonants below the vowel line." (See B II,c.2,3.) The last note of each intervallic leap should be considered a bridge to the next note (→):

ü ———— i ———— ü ———— i ———— ü
[y] [i]
ky ———— ri ———— ky ———— ri ———— ky
[y]
kö ———— re ———— kö ———— re ———— kö
[ø] [e]
ku ———— ru ———— ku ———— ru ———— ku
[u]
ky ———— rä ———— ky ———— rä ———— ky
[ʏ] [ɛ]

9. aa. Increase the intervals and the range of pitches as a "game of space." Use the vowel 'a' [a] for a natural opening of the vocal tract. Before reaching the highest tone, check the mouth opening with two fingers inserted between the teeth. The opening appropriate for 'a' [a] remains for 'i' [i] in the high range. Move the jaw gently. The tone should be "carried"— not shoved:

su ———— so ———— sa ———— so ———— su
[u] [o] [a]
su ———— sü ———— si ———— su ———— su
[y] [i]

bb.

ma ————————————— mu
[a] [y]
mü ————————————— mi
[y] [i]

10. The choir sighs. The factions of the group used for exercise 7 (above), sigh on their mixture of vowel 'u' [u], 'o' [o], 'i' [i], 'ä' [ɛ]. This exercise mixes the registers more strongly.

c. Baroque

Sound Ideal: Bright, rich in overtones, slender, intense, stream of resonance, monochromatic, martellato.

1. Relaxing and stretching the body. Thorough expulsion of air from lungs. Preparation for deep breathing: The choir stands. Stretch the arms above the head with hands folded, palms turned upward. Stretch the entire body. Roll the arms forward with hands folded; palms turned upward. Perform the same exercises behind the back. Shake the arms vigorously. Let the body shiver as if under a cold shower. Press the hands together as if grasping a hatchet. Bounce on both legs while imitating a lumberjack chopping wood. Breathe out on "tsh" [t ʃ] with each stroke. Drop forward from the waist with arms and hands dangling. Allow the breath to flow in and out easily. Notice how the back expands as the air enters the relaxed torso. Straighten the body gradually through a seep of incoming air. (Imagine the body being inflated.) Sigh. (See A I,a-c and B I,a,1-5.)

2. Diaphragmatic activation in rhythmic flexibility (without phonation) as preparation for martellato singing: A familiar tune can be used as an aid. (Relaxation and pleasure.) Work through the rhythm of a song like *Yankee Doodle* with the consonant 's' [s]. A feeling of expansion should be felt as body awaits the breath. Allow the air to fall into the body. Image: The air sweeps around the singers in the form of a ball. This opens the space into which the ball of air can circulate. Articulate the rhythm of the song in canon. The altos and basses use 's' [s] while the sopranos and tenors blast the air on 'f' [f]. (See A II,a,1-5 and B I,c,1 and 5.)

3. Connection of diaphragmatic impulses to texted sound: The path leads from dark-thick sounds to brighter-narrower ones. Maintain the sensation of breadth. "Bark" like a St. Bernard dog on a low, deep 'u' [u]; like a Spitz with a bright 'a' [a]; bleat like a goat "meh" [ɛ].

4. aa. Achieve a solid mask resonance through 'nj' [nj], 'ae' [ɛ]. Transfer this sound to the vowels 'e' [e] and 'i' [i]. Round the lips to concentrate the sound. Remember to expose the upper teeth. (See B I,j,10.) Image: Rest the forefinger under the nose. Sing through the hard palate, teeth and finger:

5. aa. It is essential to relax the jaw to produce an open, well-placed sound. The following exercise is useful for martellato technique. Sharp

diaphragm impulses and flexible jaw motion must be coordinated. (See B II,e.):

lă̆ lă̆ lă̆ (etc.)
[ɛ]
dă̆ dă̆ dă̆ "
[ɛ]
mă̆ mă̆ mă̆ "
[ɛ]

bb. Sustain only the first and second pitches:

da da da da (etc.)
[a]

cc. Slur two notes together. The first note receives a diaphragm impulse:

da__ da__ (etc.)
[a]

dd. Give the first note of the group a diaphragm impulse. Divide the second and fourth notes with a jaw motion. Transpose the exercise chromatically in higher keys. Increase the tempo:

da_____ da_____ (etc.)
[a]

6. aa. Vocal agility is enhanced through the performance of Baroque flourishes:

ni
[i]
nă̆
[ɛ]

bb.

ü
[y]
e
[e]
ă̆
[ɛ]

cc.

7. aa. To sing an intense 'piano', sing the phrase 'forte' first. The singer should feel the activity of the diaphragm. Next, alternate between 'forte' and 'piano' (7 bb). Common bad habit among choirs: 'piano' singing is limp and sluggish. The conductor should encourage the opposite by suggesting an intense and animated 'piano.' Change the pitch levels and the syllables:

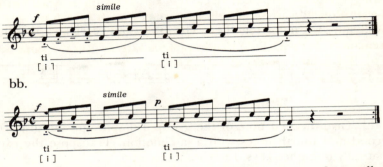

bb.

8. Sing a "laughing canon" which combines a series of martellato and staccato. The first group of notes are sung with 'i' [i], second with 'a' [a], and third with 'u' [u]:

Laughing Canon, "Ha, Ha, Ha", Traditional

d. Classic

Sound Ideal: Bouncy, flexible, individual, sensitive, extended high and low registers.

1. Relaxation and strengthening of the shoulders and back. Freedom for the throat: The choir stands. Each member turns to a neighbor and massages the back and shoulders. Chop up and down the back with the sides of the hands. Reverse the partners. Turn back to the conductor. Lift right shoulder to the ear and release with a heavy arm. Do the same with the left shoulder. Drop the head to the left and let it hang. Drop the head to

the right in the same manner. Roll the head by its own weight as if it were an apple on a thin stem. Sigh and yawn; flex the knees. Roll the shoulders in large circles. (See B I,c,1 and 2.)

2. Burst forth with a group of explosive sounds. This activity resembles a muscular massage for the diaphragm. (Use the hands to guide the abdomen.) (See B I,c,1 and 2.)

    p,t,k-p,t,k-p,t,k
    f, ss, sh-f, ss, sh-f, ss, sh
    p, t, k, f, ss, sh-p,t,k, f, ss, sh

3. Parcel out the air as the divisions of the music demands. Allow a specific interval of time for inhalation and exhalation and an interval of rest for body awareness. After inhalation, acknowledge the contribution of the rest period for deeper, more controlled breath support: Exhale the air in two long thrusts—wait—and draw the air "through a straw" in two slurps—wait. Repeat with 3,4,5,6 thrusts—sigh. (See B I,e,1-5.):

4. Wail like a siren from the low register through the high voice using the consonant 'v' [v] with little diaphragmatic activity. Do the same on 's' [s], 'n' [n], 'l' [l], 'm' [m]. (See A III,c,3.):

5. aa. The sounds (see 4 above) will be transferred to fixed pitches:

bb. Vowels are assigned to the pitches, creating tone syllables:

6. aa. French nasals obtain immediate nasal and frontal resonance. Thus, nasals are useful for teaching forward placement to amateur singers (See B I,j,10). Both exercises (6 aa. and bb.) should be sung with "flared" nostrils, as if one were smelling a rose. (See A II.) Hold the sound in the nasal region as the phrase descends; do not open the mouth too wide. Use the consonants to advantage for proper placement:

bb.

pain____ bien ___ bon _____
[ɛ̃] [ɛ̃] [ɔ̃]

7. Combining French nasals with vowels: "Place" both initial notes carefully and set the succeeding notes in the same place. Sing each eighth note lightly and easily:

bon   bien   bi bi bi (etc.)
[ɔ̃]   [ɛ̃]   [i]
don   dien   di di di   "
lon   lien   li li li   "

8. Approach coloratura singing with small intervals at a slow tempo. Begin in mezzo-piano dynamic. The jaw relaxes. Each tone requires the mental impulse of a new vowel. Increase the tempo:

[i] i____ (i) ____ (i) — (i) ____ (etc.)
    ɛ____ (ɛ) ____ (ɛ)—(ɛ) ____   "
[ɛ]

9. aa. Singing coloratura: Each note of the phrase is a pearl emitted from the relaxed jaw. Coloratura must be lighter and more elegant than the martellato of the Baroque. Think a new vowel sound for each tone. Imagine an open and receptive vocal tract:

u _____
[u]
[a]
a _____
[ɛ]

bb. Sing all the vowels at random. The tone should be more slender as the melody ascends. Do not press the sound. Image: Sing from the nape of the neck. Sigh or yawn between transposed repetitions of the exercise:

10. Create a connection between the diaphragm and the resonating center of the voice with staccato singing, ornamented by appoggiatura. Do not confuse the diaphragmatic impulse with a glottal attack. (See B II,a,1,ff.):

ü	ü	ü	(etc.)

[y]
[e]   e   e   "
[ø]   ö   ö   "
[a]   ä   ä   "
[ε]

11. Alternate long notes with coloratura figures. Precision for the coloratura will be enhanced if the long note ends in a slight decrescendo. The diaphragm relaxes. (See B II,e,20 and 21.) With this relaxation, the coloratura flourish will flow easily and clearly. Imagine a new vowel for the first sixteenth note of each group:

di ____ (i) _____ (i) _____ (i) _____

12. Combine the extremes of high and low. Sing the pitches in the low register with bright vowels (consistency of registers), taking the higher notes "in stride". Sing the low register lightly, the higher passage with depth. The ascending line is sung rapidly. The jaw gives way to additional space for the last third:

[i]
[ä] _____
[e]   [a] _____

13. Frequency of consonants: Speak the consonants and then sing them on one pitch level. Assign pitches to the exercise. Increase the tempo so that the line achieves a playful, flexible character:

du ru ku (etc.)
[u]
ki pi ti "
[i]
pa fa ta "
[a]
ky - ri - e "
glo- ri - a "

e. Romantic

Sound Ideal: Dark, supple, warm, round, wide, intimate, expressive; fluctuation of sound for dynamic contrast.

1. Additions to Breathing Technique: The choir remains seated. The singers may lay their scores on the floor. Ask them to sprawl across their chairs, sighing, rolling head and shoulders. Leaning back on the chair with eyes closed, listen inwardly. Silence ensues. Each singer breathes at their own rate as if asleep: Air streams out quickly (mouth)—a period of rest—the air falls into the body slowly (nose)—a period of rest—the air escapes swiftly. During exhalation, the lips vibrate the explosive consonant group "ph" [f]. (See B I,d,2.)

2. For building resonance, rest the lips gently together and strike up a low hum-like groaning sound (like thunder grumbling in the distance). Lay both hands along the cheekbones and groan into them m--u--m--u (like a cow). Increase the speaking voice and interpolate other vowels such as 'm' - 'u' [u],-'o' [o],- 'a' [a], etc.

3. Pendulum motion: Sway with the head and torso from side to side. Close the eyes (promoting a sensation of slumber). Sing "in the mask": the vowel is initiated with a short 'b' [b] (clapper of the bell), and "hurled" into the mask, where a long "m" [m] catches and spins forth the sound. (See B II,j,8 and 9):

4. Games in chordal sounds awaken the harmonic consciousness. Sit upright with eyes open. Continue to sway (As in e,3 above) and produce a chord with the consonant 'm' [m] (lips easily together such that the humming creates a tickling sensation); expand the sound from pianissimo to mezzo forte. (Remain in the middle octave of the range. The consonant 'm' [m] causes tension when sung in high passages.) The exercise can be performed with 'ng' [ŋ] and can be transposed to various keys and chordal inversions. (The jaw should hang.):

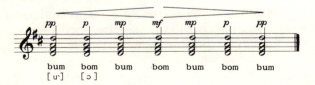

5. A canon for mixed voices will elevate the feeling for harmony. The canon melody follows from syllables of explosive and sustained consonants ('b', 'm') to rounded vowel sounds. Divide the group into three parts; apply the arched mouth formation of 'u' [u] and 'o' [o] for the vowel 'a' [a]. The

opening for 'a' [a] is slightly larger, however. The choir stands, swaying from side to side while singing:

Bell Canon, "Horch, Es Toent", Traditional

6. Amplify the sound to 'forte'. Nod the head lightly. Place a finger between the eyebrows. Sing 'u' [u] in piano dynamic; feel the sound between the eyes, then "pull the sound back over the head." At the highest position over the head, make a large circular motion while increasing the volume of the pitch from 'piano' to 'forte' without applying any pressure ("halo" of sound). The hand motion helps to amplify the sound by widening the space rather than by employing muscular force:

7. Broaden the sound horizontally (not the mouth!). As in Exercise 6, widen the singer's fishmouth from the vowel 'u' [u] to 'o' [o] and then to 'a' [a] resulting in a crescendo. Using both hands, stretch the head as if it were a balloon being filled slowly with air (or use the image of an accordion). Repeat by stretching the throat:

8. Reduce the sound. Acquire a decrescendo by reversing the hand motions of exercise e,7 above. Imagine the deflation of a balloon or the closing of an accordion:

9. Addition of brighter vowels. Again begin with 'u' [u]; retain the oval mouth formation for the 'e' [e] and 'i' [i]. Lead the vowel pattern from 'i' [i] to 'u' [u] again:

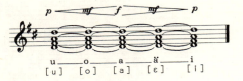

10. Distribution of the dynamic phrase to short note values. If the crescendo-decrescendo does not occur consistently (generally the dynamic gradations transpire too quickly), subdivide the note values. This practice will assist the singers in increasing and decreasing the sound in smaller units. By longer note values, the singer must think the pulsations of shorter values so that the progression from pianissimo to fortissimo can be steady:

Exercises e,9 and 10 can be transposed. Use minor keys also.

11. Application of dynamic principle to a legato line. Before singing, sigh on the vowel 'u' [u] arriving as close as possible to the first pitch of the phrase. (See C I,a,5.):

12.

13. Sing a melodic period with different dynamic indications for each phrase. Take in the breath with a feeling for width, sigh on 'u' [u]; catch a

breath in the middle. (A long crescendo, a short decrescendo, etc.) Slow tempo:

lu   lu   lu (etc.)
[u]
so   so   so   "
[o]

14. Repetition of exercise e,13. The tenors and basses accompany the treble voices with a two-measure bourdon. The bourdon repeats, adhering to the dynamic changes of the treble melody:

Bourdon: mom mom mom (etc.)
         [ɔ]
        bam bam bam "
        [ʌ]

f. Modern, avant-garde

Sound Ideal: hard, cool, objective; tension from sensibility to brutality; extreme shifts of dynamic; development of high and low sound regions; rapid changes; ecstasy.

The sound of avant-garde music grew from the "Heldenoper" (heroic opera)— *(Tristan and Isolde, Moses and Aaron).* The music calls for voices of great magnitude (Heldentenor). This music has influenced other archetypes (church music, basic musical training systems). It is helpful to address the technical demands of avant-garde repertoire from the vantage point of the Bel Canto School.

1. Relaxation of the whole body: The choir stands. Shake out all the extremities; flex the knees; swivel the pelvic region from right to left; shrug the shoulders; nod the head in affirmation and in negation. Sigh. Fold the arms over the abdomen and expel the air instantly on 'tsh' [t ʃ]. Spread the arms to encourage expansion as the breath rushes into the body. Repeat the entire pattern. Sigh. (See A I,a-c.)

2. aa. Activation of the diaphragm as basis for breath support. Lift the breastbone and blast the air intensely. (See B I,c,1.):

cc. Develop a crescendo by intensifying diaphragmatic activity:

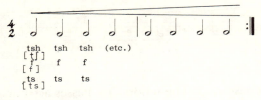

tsh   tsh   tsh   (etc.)
[tʃ]
[f]   f   f
ts   ts   ts
[ts]

dd.

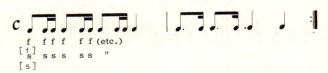

f   f f f   f f (etc.)
[f]
s   s s s   s s   "
[s]

3. aa. Connection between diaphragm impulse and speech sounds: Repeat the vowel sounds at a medium speaking level without interrupting the tonal stream. Supply each sound with a diaphragm pressure, like a bark from a dog. (See B II,a,3 and 4.):

u   u   u   u   (etc.)
[u]

bb.

p   u   u   u   u
mf [u]
    o   o   o
f   [o]
    a   a   a
    [a]

4. Glide the voice from pitch to pitch driving the sound forward with accents. Wail like a siren from above and carry the voice back to the starting pitch. Accentuate the shifts of directions. The registers are mixed in this manner:

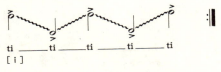

ti ——— ti ——— ti ——— ti ——— ti
[i]

5. With the mouth wide open (position for 'a' [a]) breathe in and out loudly. Gradually close the mouth by subsequent inhalations so that from

an 'o' [o], an 'u' [u] sound results. As the progress concludes, only the sound 'ch' [ç] remains.

6. Imitate the shriek of an angry swan, using the consonant group 'ch' [ç] combined with a diaphragmatic impulse. (See B I,i,1.)

7. Pretend to frighten someone in a dark room; utter groaning sounds of several colors (always in connection with the diaphragm); dynamics from 'p-f':

8. aa. Support diaphragmatic impulses with sharp consonants. Hit the sound with an explosive consonant and a diaphragm pressure simultaneously (bell). Direct this coordination with a hand on the abdominal wall:

ti   ta   to   (etc.)
[i] [a] [o]

bb.

ti ___ i ___ i   tä ___ ä ___ ä   tö ___ ö ___ ö   ti ___ i ___ i   tä ___ ä ___ ä
[i]   [ε]   [ø]   [i]   [ε]

cc. Call syllables through a megaphone formed by the hands cupped about the mouth:

mf   *f*   *ff*

ti ~~~ to ~~~ ta ~~~
[i] [o] [a]

9. Creating width and tonal energy: The image of calling opens the vocal tract and stretches the breath mechanism, thus increasing the power of the sound. In exercise 9 the 'a' [a] acquires high forward placement from the 'd' [d] and 'i' [i]. Articulate the consonants with flexibility. Pause for the air to fall deep into the body. (See A III,e,4.):

di -a di -a di -a   (etc.)
[i][a]
ti -a ti -a ti -a   "
[i][a]

10. Security for initial attacks. Listen to the pitches of the descending scale before singing; follow the lowest tones. Lead the gliding motions from the diaphragm. The jaw should be relaxed. Accelerate the tempo. Include all intervening tones for the slides at the end (wail):

11. Developing the low register diatonically with mask resonance. An intensely sung 'nj' [nj] combination provides high and forward placement, awakes mask resonance and gives color to the tone.(See B I,j,7,bb and cc.) The 'a' [a] must maintain this placement in the low register also. Steady management of the descending passage is essential. Remember to direct the mind to a line in contrary motion.(See B I,k,3,aa.) Transpose downward chromatically. Use the hands as a loud speaker for resonance. Refrain from a wide mouth opening:

12. aa. Reach facility in the high voice by a buoyant line of the sound over a broken chord. Relax the jaw. Afford the first of each sixteenth group a diaphragmatic impulse. Widen the vocal tract for the highest tone. Advance the exercise upward in chromatic progressions. Altos and basses may not be able to proceed through all the transpositions. Flex the knees when approaching the highest tones. (See B II, b4.):

bb.

13. Interpolate appropriate tone syllables into familiar songs creating calls. An open body and vocal tract are acquired through life-related images, without burdening the throat for 'forte' passages. (See A III,e,4.) Form a megaphone with the hands. Imagine sending the sound through the opposite wall. Call into the forest and listen for an echo. (See A III,e,4,aa.) Improvise with chordal variations. Choose a song with a call as part of its text. Increase the volume:

```
hal - lo,        hal - lo,        hal - lo_____
[ a ][ o ]
hol - la,        hol - la,        hol - la _____
[ ɔ ][ a ]
```

14. The rolled 'r' [r] as the coachman sound. Further strengthening of the diaphragm and activation of support. Chromatic transpositions. Also scales:

```
r_____          r_____          r_____
brh_____        brh_____        brh_____
```

15. Scales cause the voice to move as well as to ease the adjustments between the registers. (See B I,d.) Relax the jaw. Transpose in all keys:

```
i _____
[ i ]
```

16. Despite the progression into lower registers, the vowels must maintain a bright coloration and a high focus of resonance:

```
i
[ i ]_____
a
[ ɛ ]_____
```

17. Chordal Call: Call energetically; sing with "wonder" and "astonishment" (open feeling). (See A III,e,4). Repeat 'piano' with the same intensity:

```
f   du      do      da      dä      di
    [ u ]   [ o ]   [ a ]   [ ɛ ]   [ i ]
p   du      do      da      dä      di
```

18. aa. Tuning exercises help to develop tonal sense. The singer is forced to hear the tones before phonating. This heightened awareness achieves a more blended choral sound. In 18 aa and bb, various segments of the choir call to the conductor at several pitch levels. In 18 cc and dd, all voices move in parallel motion. It can be helpful to have the beginning and final chord played on a keyboard instrument. Thereby the choir is conscious of its goal and its key relation. Stagger the breath so that the chordal stream is not interrupted:

bb.

cc.

dd.

19. Develop a cluster. The basses begin on 'du' [u] in the low register. Each singer sings a tone which is slightly higher than the one sung by a neighbor. (Stagger breathing throughout.) After all the basses have selected pitches in this manner, move on to the tenors, altos and sopranos. Every singer tries to hold "the" tone resisting those of neighbors. This tonal

structure can be adjusted upwards or downwards. Change the vowels. Make dynamic differences.

20. Develop a cluster in half steps. Divide the choir into groups, mixing Alto and Bass, Soprano and Tenor. Give the lowest group a pitch and add the other sections one at a time by ascending half steps. Each group should hold its respective pitch until the entire cluster is formed.

II. WARM-UP EXERCISES FOR SPECIAL PROBLEMS IN SPECIFIC CHORAL WORKS

The exercises are developed from the respective composition. Unless indicated, all exercises should be transposed to keys above and below the given examples. In each case, a few movements of an oratorio will be extracted for consideration. It is assumed that one will transfer the principles to similar technical difficulties in other sections of the work.

a. *Dancing and Springing,* Hans Leo Hassler

Objective: Flexibly supported, precise phonation—'forte' and 'piano'.

1. aa. "Blast" the rhythm of the first phrase (in a simplified form) on [f]. Give intense diaphragm impulses. Begin 'forte' and repeat 'piano'. Both should have the same intensity and vibrance:

bb. Do the same on 'ss' [s].

2. aa. Speak the rhythm of the song version with the jaw and the diaphragm in easy coordination:

bb. Speak the rhythm on "fa la la," giving a gentle diaphragmatic impulse on the first beat of each measure.

3. Sing Exercise 2 aa above on one pitch first 'forte' and then 'piano'. Do not move the jaw (hold the chin with a hand if necessary) so that the tongue can move actively. Give the same diaphragmatic support as described in 2 bb above:

4. Perform as in exercise a,3 above but with flexible jaw action. Be certain that the exercise maintains the same intensity 'piano' that it had 'forte.'

5. All the singers sing the soprano part of the first phrase (transpose to a medium key, perhaps g-major) "fa la la."

6. Singers sing their respective parts of the first phrase on "fa la la."

7. Each singer on their own part sings the entire piece on "fa la la."

8. Speak only the vowels of the text in rhythm. Place a 'd' before each tone (deh, di, deh, di, di, etc.). Sing the syllables on one tone in the rhythm of the piece.

9. Prepare for the quick and exact articulation of the consonants of the text, first by speaking them and then by singing them on one tone. Each syllable receives a diaphragm pressure:

Dan - cing and sprin - ging, sin - ging and rin - ging

10. Sing the entire setting; repeat as an echo. Draw a phrase marking over each line, minimizing the diaphragm impulses on the first beat of each measure.

b. *Lobe den Herrn*, Hugo Distler

Objective: Bright, elastic, sensitive sound; catch breaths as standard throughout.

1. Use French nasal sounds to develop the bright vowels and to encourage mask resonance. (See B I,j,10):

bien   bä bä   bi —— bi
[ɛ̃]   [ɛ]   [i]

2. Control the consonants from the diaphragm. Drop the jaw for each leap of a fifth. Each tone dances on the diaphragm like a bouncing tennis ball. (See B II,a,9.):

dü dü dü (etc.)
[y]
dä di dä   "
[ɛ][i]
di da di   "
[i][a]

3. Sing in light loose parlando style:

na   na na   na (etc.)
[a]

4. Connect the eighth-note chains, but do not smear. Imagine a new vowel for each tone; relax the jaw. (See B II,c,7.):

5. Snatch a breath. Open the body in "amazement" during each eighth-note rest and allow the air to fall into the body silently:

6. Use the technique for rapid breath intake (defined in 5) for the following exercise, whereby the eighth-note rest before each breath mark is shortened to a sixteenth note:

c. *De profundis*, Josquin des Prez

Objective: Quiet flowing, consistent sound; little vibrato, legato line.

1. Exhale slowly on 'f' [f]. Imagine that the back is stretched to its fullest length. Repeat on 's' [s].

2. Sustain a sounding 'l'; rest the tip of the tongue lightly on the upper teeth:

3. Transfer the sound of the 'l' (head voice) to the 'u':

4. Include vowels with larger mouth space 'a' [a], 'o' [o]. Draw all the vowels to the position where the 'u' [u] has been placed:

5. Repeat Exercise 4 with bright vowels.

6. Transpose this exercise by half steps up to F major. Transpose down to G major. An alternative ending is indicated for sopranos and tenors. The choir sings very legato and cantabile. The diaphragmatic impulses must not protrude from a melodic phrase. Think a new vowel sound for each tone of the melismas. (See B II,c,7.):

7. Sing the last series of notes with intense legato connection. Articulate the consonants quickly and precisely. (See B II,c,21.) Listen for the last tone of the series as the melody begins. Sing toward the cadence throughout. Anticipate the fifth and octave skips by imagining the motion in the opposite directions. Demonstrate the flow of sound with a gesture of the hand. Emphasize the lower registers by each consecutive transposition:

d. *Lobet den Herrn, alle Heiden*, Johann Sebastian Bach

Objective: brighter, more flexible sound; high register; fluctuation between martellato and legato.

1. Pant like a dog.

2. Bark like a dog on 'u' [u] and 'ü' [y].

3. The diaphragm pushes of exercise 2 above are applied to staccato singing. (See B II,a):

4. Combine staccato and martellato:

5. Expand the tonal range in staccato; retain a loose jaw. The highest tone of each exercise requires the largest opening of the vocal tract, even if a narrow vowel [e] or [i], etc. is to be sung. Transpose the exercise to higher keys. (See B II,b,1.):

6. See exercise 5 above: Combine the staccato singing with martellato patterns:

7. Begin slowly, increase the tempo. Imagine a new vowel sound for each new note. Separate the eighth notes with small jaw motions. (See B II, e,12aa.):

8. Contrary to the exercises d,3-7 above, hold the diaphragm still, sing legato cantabile (measures 58 ff.):

9. Animate each new tone with messa di voce (a tension and relaxation of the sound, i.e., crescendo-decrescendo). Lean forward from the waist to

encourage the effect. (See B II,e,21 and 22.):

10. Use the messa di voce technique to shape the figure below: loose jaw, small intense diaphragm pressures. Expand the body for the octave jumps (astonishment), allow the air to drop into the body cavity with a catch breath. Think deeply for the octave skip (measures 99 ff.):

11. Sing the melismatic figures as described in exercise 10 above, first on a syllable and then to the appropriate text:

e. *Locus iste*, Anton Bruckner

Objective: dark, warm, full sound; greater dynamic contrast from pianissimo to fortissimo, strengthening of high and low registers.

1. The lips are "thick" and rest on each other. Hum with the sensation that the jaw is suspended from the cheekbones. (The lips should tickle.) Imagine the formation for the vowel 'u' [u]; sing legato, cantabile. (See B II,j,2,dd.):

2. Set the 'l' between the eyes. Allow the vowel 'u' [u] to develop from the same focal point. (See B II,j,3.):

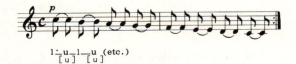

3. Amplification of sound through vowel modification. (See B II,d,7.):

4. Crescendo and decrescendo on the vowel 'a' [a]. In each succeeding measure simply imagine the vowel sound indicated in parentheses. Notice the dilation and contraction of the vocal tract. Resist any pressure. (See B II,d,7 and 8.):

5. Crescendo-decrescendo by conceiving vowel modification in a harmonic context: Avoid breath pressure on the throat during dynamic exercises. Expansion for each vowel prevents excess tension. (See 3-5 above.):

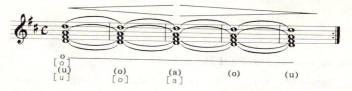

6. Sing the highest tone as well as the vowels 'eh' [ɛ] and 'i' [i] with the mouth formation for the open 'a' [a]. (Measure 7, 8, 36, 38):

7. The vowel 'ä' [ɛ] loses its forward placement easily in the higher tessitura. As the phrase moves above c′, the singers (particularly the women's voices) should either modify to an 'e' [e] or an 'i' [i] vowel in order to remove the indefinite sound of 'ä' [ɛ]:

8. Freer vowel attack. Attack the vowels with a small jaw motion. There should be no glottal stop before the vowel. Imagine an aspirate 'h' as an emergency aid:

9. Select syllables from the text of the motet for exercises with open vowel attacks. (See e,8 above.):

10. Sing with open space. Think about breadth in the sound. Maintain the same intensity for the 'pianissimo' dynamic as for the 'forte':

f. *O musica, du edle Kunst,* **Paul Peuerl**

Objective: Brighter, wider, "beckoning" sound, flexible consonant articulation, shift from polyphonic networks to homophonic planes of sound.

1. The hands form a megaphone about the mouth. Call through the hands, opening the vocal tract. Slide up and down chromatically:

2. See exercise f,1 above:

3. Extension of f,2 above. The octave leap should be approached with a feeling of depth. (See B I,k,3,aa.):

4. Maintain width in the vocal tract. The sopranos should sing the 'u' [u] through the 'a' [a] mouth form:

5. Speak sharp consonants with the help of energetic diaphragm pushes:

6. Sing tone syllables with the diaphragmatic intensity achieved in f,5 above:

7. See exercise f,6 above:

8. Combine both styles of singing. (See f,3,7 above.):

9. See f,5 above. For the text "dann du viel Lust," employ light diaphragmatic impulses:

O mu - si -ca, o mu - si - ca
[o] [u] [i][a]
simile

dann du viel Lust und Kurz - weil bringst
[a] [u] [i] [u] [u] [u] [æ] [i][ɔ]st]

g. *Messiah*, George Frederick Handel

1. "His yoke is easy" (#21)

Objective: Bright sound, rich in overtones; martellato technique, melismatic passages and rapid coloraturas.

a. Prepare for martellato with flexible jaw motion and diaphragm pushes (measure 1, 2). "Blast" the rhythm, first in a slow tempo accompanied by clapping:

f f f f (etc.)
s s s s s "

b. Speak the rhythm with a flexible jaw:

da   da da (etc.)
[a]

c. Sing the rhythm on one tone. Add the diaphragm pushes practiced during exercise g,l,a above:

simile

da   da da (etc.)
[a]
di   di di (etc.)
[i]

d. The melismatic phrases of this movement cause sluggish forward motion if not carefully performed. Consider the following exercises:

Begin with each tone of the sixteenth-note groups receiving a diaphragm pressure. Accelerate the tempo:

simile

da   da —— da   da —— (etc.)   da
[a]

e. Tie the first note of each sixteenth-note group but retain the diaphragm pressure. Relax the diaphragm by the quarter-note (messa di voce, see glossary of terms):

f. Change the rhythm:

g. Sing the theme of the soprano part at measure 16. A diaphragmatic impulse accents the major beats while a gentle motion of the jaw separates the smaller divisions of the beat. Maintain the focus of the 'i' for the darker vowels of the next:

h. The second part of the theme calls for an opening of the vocal tract to accommodate the leaps of a sixth. Crescendo the fourth tone of the phrase and increase mouth space before the large intervallic skip (measures 3-5). Transpose the segment until the soprano and tenor voices reach b' as the highest pitch:

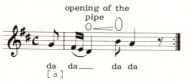

2. **"Behold the Lamb of God" (#22)**

Objective: Legato with double-dotted articulation; octave leaps; tonal repetitions; vowel modification.

a. Sing each note with a portato diaphragm impulse (not as sharp as for martellato). The vowels are of equal length. Envision the end of the phrase from the outset. Guide the voice to the cadence:

b. Use the same procedure as of g,2a above, applying the principles to dotted rhythms:

do do do (etc.)
[o]

c. Begin the melodic fragment with an octave leap as written. Imagine the disparate pitches to be sung on the same pitch level as in g,2a and b above:

de da de da (etc.)
[e][a]

d. Practice the initial theme of the movement with all the singers at a moderate pitch level. Thereafter, transpose the phrase upward for the sopranos and tenors. Repeat in lower keys for the altos and basses:

Be -hold the lamb of God the lamb of God

e. The singers should counter the monotony of tonal repetitions by ascending hand gestures to encourage accurate intonation. (Measure 17 ff.):

du du du (etc.)
[u]

f. Supply the vowel series from the text, closing the open vowel sounds where appropriate. (See c 27bb):

da da de da de da di da da do
[a] [a] [ε][a][e] [a] [i] [a] [a][o]

g. Add the complete sentence:

that ta - keth a - way the sins of the world
[a] [e] [ə][a] [e] [ɔ] [i] [ɔ] [ə] [ɔ]

h. The sopranos should use the mouth position of 'a' [a] for all 'e' [e] vowels in the upper register, mixing 'e' [e] and 'eh' [ɛ]:

i. Apply the sound of the 'e' [e] and 'i' [i] combination to the word "world:"

3. **"Surely He hath borne our griefs" (#24)**

Objective: Call 'forte'; legato; expressive consonants.

a. The hands form a megaphone. Allow the breath to fall into the body. Support the calls with diaphragmatic impulses:

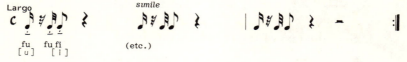

b. Perform in the same way as the previous exercise:

c. As in exercise g 3,b above, sing the text to the movement on one note. The diaphragm assists the articulation of the consonant 's'. Only imagine the rests in the actual context of the performance:

d. Select other melodic fragments from the music to be sung with similar intensity. Call and sing them:

e. In preparation for a legato line, do not interrupt the stream of resonance with the consonants. Each vowel should be sung as long as possible:

f. Use the vowel pattern of the text. Image: One vowel continues to sound as the next one is phonated:

g. Speak the consonants from the diaphragm with energy. They are useful for underscoring the meaning of the words:

b—*b*orne; *gr*—*gr*iefs; *k*—*c*arried; *s*—*s*orrows

h. Sing these words with "energetic" consonants. Image: The listeners are deaf and must read the text from the singer's lips. Divide the consonants from the vowels to illustrate the equality of the verbal sounds. Sing the passage as an exercise:

i. Sing the text of the theme on one tone:

Measure 13 ff will be taught in the same manner.

4. "All we like sheep have gone astray" (#26)

Objective: 'Forte' calling sounds in high and low registers; legato and martellato vocalises.

a. Develop an expanded body awareness for measures 1-3, 6-8, 11, 23, 24, etc. The sopranos and tenors sing with the images used for teaching the soprano line and the altos and basses for the bass line—repeat the passage an octave lower with twice the intensity:

na na   na   na   nee nee nee   nee

b. Complete the melodic fragment taught in g,4,a above with a different and even character (measures 11, 23, etc.). All the singers sing the bass version. Image: the octave is sung on the same pitch level:

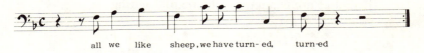

all we   like   sheep, we have turn- ed,   turn-ed

c. Sing the alto version from measure 34/35 as a canon. This will help the successive entrances of the choir to occur organically. Each singer takes the tempo and phrase direction from the preceding singer's adaptation:

naw naw naw naw
[aʊ]
have gone a - stray
[ɛ] [ɔ][a] [e]

d. The vocalises of measures 19,22,40,41,56-59 must be sung as a very legato sixteenth-note martellato chain. The singers should imagine the recurring vowels as new entities. Each vowel is treated with a small jaw movement. This practice will avoid the tendency to smear repeated notes:

dŏ dŏ dŏ (etc.)
[ɔ]

e. Sing the second part of the theme on one syllable using the method for tonal repetition described in g,4,d above:

do do do do do   deh (eh) (etc.)
[o]   [ɛ]

f. Use preparatory exercises g,1, a-d for the precision required for the sixteenth-note chain at measures 11-14, 23-26, 42-45, 65-70:

g. The sopranos are expected to sing a syllabic text at a high pitch level in measure 27-28. Sing the melody on 'na' [a] first. Repeat immediately with the text. The position of the vocal tract (i.e., that of the vowel 'a' [a]) should not change for the textual setting:

5. "Lift up your heads, o ye gates" (#33)

Objective: Bright 'forte' calling sound; clear, intense pronunciation; double choir effect; messa di voce in vocalises.

a. For exercises addressing the 'forte' calling sound, see g,3,a-e. Practice the following double choir exercise: SI, SII, A and ATB call to one another with a bright 'i' [i] sound as guide. 'njeh' [ɲie] involves forward placement:

b. Often choral singers are accustomed to eliding end consonants with the succeeding word. Example: Lif-tup-your heads. Add the exercise for careful enunciation:

> Shape the mouth for the first vowel, breathe, speak the first syllable (or the word) and shape the mouth suddenly to form the next vowel—rest—repeat:
> lift up = lift (position mouth for 'u' [ʌ])—up
> king of = king (position mouth for 'o' [ɔ])—of
> come in = come (position mouth for 'i' [i])—in
> lord of = lord (position mouth for 'o' [ɔ])—of

c. Sing the exercises which have been spoken:

<pre>
king (a) of
come (i) in
Lord (a) of
Lift (u) up
</pre>

d. Sing through the text, imagining the rests between the end consonants and the next words. Proper articulation of end consonants will help in clarifying certain textual phrases:

king | of,   come | in,   Lord | of   Hosts

e. Build the principles of good pronunciation as they relate to the textual meaning. The diaphragm supports the calling character of the words:

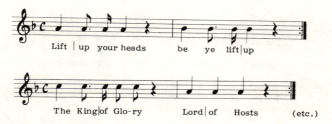

Lift | up your heads   be   ye lift|up

The King|of Glo-ry   Lord|of   Hosts   (etc.)

f. Rhythmic accuracy can be gained when the martellato technique is augmented by messa di voce singing. This method is described in detail at g,1,a-g (measures 43 ff.). Clap the rhythm while singing the following exercise. Allow the singers to take turns with each repetition. Sing the exercise such that each dotted note is sustained through its full value:

6. **"The Lord gave the Word; Great was the company of the preachers"** (#37)

Objective: Parlando; precise articulated vocalises; vowel modification.

a. Whisper the text on one tone with loose jaw motions and an evenly rounded mouth opening:

Great was the com - pa-ny of the prea - chers

b. Call out 'forte': "The Lord gave the Word!" Sing the text on one note with the identical character:

Call: The Lord gave the word:

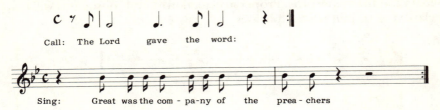

Sing: Great was the com - pa-ny of the prea - chers

c. Sing both texts: reduce the volume of sound after the calling segment. The parlando passage begins softly, repeating the syllables quickly:

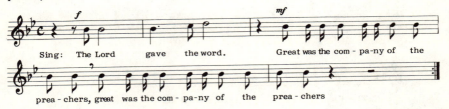

Sing: The Lord gave the word. Great was the com - pa-ny of the

prea - chers, great was the com - pa-ny of the prea - chers

d. Practice martellato for the sixteenth-note vocalises as defined in g,1,a-d; g,4,ff (measures 17 ff.). Begin in the lower register and advance upward. The singer should start with a small, rounded mouth opening. For the vowel 'o' [ɔ] of "company," open the vowel to 'a' [a]. The higher the exercise, the more the jaw should fall, opening the vocal tract. The vowel 'o' [ɔ] modifies to 'a' [a]. When the sopranos and tenors move above c', they should mix the vowel 'u' [u] into the vowel 'a' [a]:

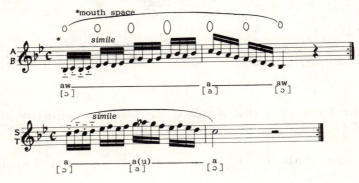

7. "Their sound is gone out" (#39)

"Objective: 'Forte' calling sound; vowel modification.
a. Use the exercises of g,3,a-e above for the strong calling quality of this setting. Begin with melodic fragment from the first section of the piece. The sopranos alternate between 'da' [a] and 'du' [u] when asked to sing above b'. If the mouth approximates the opening for the 'a' [a] vowel, more head sound will be provided. During the repetition, the singers should alternate between 'u' [u] and the 'a' [a], placing the 'u' [u] in the 'a' [a] space:

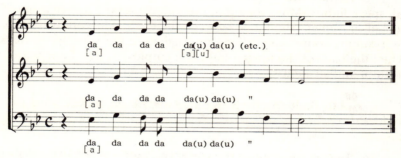

b. Treat the vowel in "ends of the world" (measure 12 ff.) as designated in the remarks and exercises of g,6,c above.

8. "Hallelujah" (#44)

Objective: Portato and legato; flexible tongue articulation of 'l'.
a. The various types of diaphragmatic involvement required by this movement must be made apparent to the choir. Blast the rhythm on 'f':

b. Execute the following rhythm with an intense crescendo. The pentultimate note is the goal!:

c. Combine exercises a and b:

110

d. Activate the jaw and the tongue simultaneously:

bla bla bla bla (etc.)
[a]
la la la la "
[a]
[a]

e. Move the tongue by itself. Open the mouth to 'a' [a]. Hold the jaw with the hand. Rest the tip of the tongue on the upper lip. Flex the tongue back and forth against the upper and lower lips rapidly.

f. Retract the tongue, holding the jaw stationary. Speak "la-la-la" [a]; speak lightly. Move the tip of the tongue as far forward as possible. Its field of movement should be between the teeth. The conductor can accept the resulting sound only when the singers use the very tip of the tongue. When the back of the tongue has been employed, the 'a' [a] sound will be guttural and strident:

la la la (etc.)
[a]

g. In order to control the vowel coloration of the first syllable of the word "hallelujah": The singer should imagine a single 'l' before each of the middle syllables.

Think of the last syllable 'jah' as an elongated vowel so that it does not sound "ripped" from the fabric of the music. Allow the breath to fall into the body quickly. Repeat the exercise often:

la la la la, hal - le - lu - ja
[a] [a][ε][u] [a]
sung: ha -le - lu - ja

h. Combine legato and portato singing. Reduce the volume of sound for the florid notes. Because the movement is long and rather redundant in its repetition of the word "hallelujah", the singers may tighten as the work progresses. Be alert to this danger:

du du du du du du al -le - lu - ja, hal -le - lu - ja
[u]
dä dä dä dä dä dä al -le - lu - ja, hal -le - lu - ja
[ε]

h. *Mass in d-minor "Lord Nelson," Franz Joseph Haydn*
Typical problems have been excerpted for the following examples.
The general methods can be applied to similar troublesome passages.

1. "Kyrie"

Objective: bright, transparent sound; octave jumps; syllabic delineation.

a. Sigh through the vowels from head voice through the lower registers. Each singer begins as high as possible (See B I,k,5):

b. Sigh from a determinate pitch level:

c. Speak the consonants accurately with a bounce of support from the diaphragm:

d. Conceive the consonants as a kind of ornament to the vowel it precedes. The consonant occurs before the beat, so that the vowel can be phonated on the beat (See B II,c,29 and 30):

Note: If a German pronunciation of Church Latin is used, the 'y' of "Kyrie" will be spoken 'ü' [y]. If the Italian pronunciation is favored, the vowel will be 'i' [i].

e. These spoken exercises are sung to specific pitches:

f. Sing the following segment with the diaphragm activity described in h, 1, c-e above. Open the mouth as the pitch level rises. Divide clearly between the vowels 'i' [i] and 'ö' [ə]:

g. Establish the vowel 'i' [i] as a point of reference for the hidden 'ä' [ɛ] of "eleison." 'i' [i] heightens the point of focus, giving the 'ä' [ɛ] more character and better resonance. (Measure 20, etc.):

h. Repeat the preceding exercise with its corresponding text from the *Mass*. The 'e' [i] vowel becomes the scaffolding upon which the other vowels are placed. The sopranos shape their mouths for an open 'a' [a] in the high register:

i. Sing the eighth notes staccato (supported by diaphragm impulses) as if they were sixteenth-notes. The effect should be graceful, not abrupt:

2. "Laudamus te"

Objective: Sforzato

a. The diaphragm should be activated in speech first. The 'tsh' [t ʃ] is given as an intense an impulse as the other consonants. (Measures 33-37):

b. 'Nudge' the tone syllables with a flexible diaphragm; then draw the vowel through the area of the consonants in decrescendo:

c. The intensity of the diaphragm remains the same as the respective syllables of the text are interpolated:

da   di   ra   ka   te
[a]   [i]   [a]   [a]   [e]

d. These spoken syllables will be sung with identical energy:

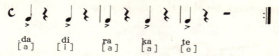

da   di   ra   ka   te
[a]   [i]   [a]   [a]   [e]

e. Transfer the sforzati to their contexts within the composition:

Lau - da -   mus te,   be - ne -di - ci - mus te
[aɔ] [a]   [u] [ɛ]   [ɛ] [ɛ][i]   [tʃi] [u] [ɛ]

3. "Quoniam tu solus Sanctus"

Objective: Supple eighth-note movement, octave jumps; martellato (measures 68-70, 77-80).

a. The jaw drops easily for each broken chord. (See B I, f,1 and 3):

na na na (etc.)
[a]
ba ba ba   "
[a]

b. Sing exercise h,3,a above on a sustained vowel with appropriate jaw action:

[a]   -   -   men
[a]   [ə]

c. The entire group sings the alto line in a simplified version without the octave leaps:

na na na (etc.)
[a]

    d. Completion of exercise h,3,c above. Sing it with the octave leaps as written. The singers pretend that the passage flows as before. The octaves remain on the same pitch level as the conjunct strides of the simplified version. (See B I, c 13):

men,a - men
[ə]

    e. Tenor and bass lines form the foundation for the soprano and alto lines in which each half note receives a diaphragmatic impulse (Measures 77-80):

men, a - - (etc.)
[ə] [a]

men, a - - (etc.)
[ə] [a]

4. "Sanctus"

Objective: Crescendo-decrescendo; piano-forte.
    a. Lay the tip of the tongue behind the incisor teeth. Focus on 'l' 'piano' "between the eyes." Increase and diminish the sound. Begin with a tiny mouth opening 'u' [u]. Open gradually to an 'a' [a] creating a crescendo. Return the mouth to the 'u' position again. There is no pressure placed upon the throat. Image: The head widens like a "water balloon" and shrinks again. Breath support. (See B I, j,8aa.). (Measures 1-6):

    b. Repeat the exercise h,4,a above beginning immediately with 'a' [a]. Imagine the vowel and mouth gradations as in exercise h,4,a above:

c. Subject the word "Sanctus" to similar treatment. Maintaining the integrity of the vowel, cause the sound to increase and diminish. Insert the consonants swiftly before the syllable "us."

d. Shorten the time frame for the crescendo-decrescendo sequence. (Measures 1-6):

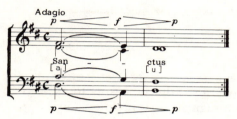

e. In order to preserve the intensity and color of the sound for sudden dynamic changes (subito p), sing the phrase 'forte' first (Measures 5-10). Retain the feeling of calling. The diaphragm should react to each consonant. (See B I, c,bb):

f. The last measure retains its intensity even when sung softly, as in exercise h,4,e above):

5. "Osanna in excelsis"

Objective: Staccato; martellato; crescendo (Measures 136 ff).

a. The functions of the diaphragm will be reinforced. The rhythm of the alto phrase:

b. Sing the rhythm on one note at a moderate tempo: first staccato, then martellato. (See B II,e,20, bb and cc.):

Exaggerate the differences between these singing techniques.

c. Add the vowels of the text to the rhythm practiced in exercise h,5,b above:

d. Using Exercise h,5 as a basis, execute Exercises a-c with the text of the passage. Bind the first note of the third measure to its preceding note value, but continue the diaphragmatic accentuation. (See C II, g,2, g-i.) Enunciate the text of the first measure briskly, as if the tones were marked staccato. Each syllable is detached from the others. (Fanfare melody: The first measure is sung as "upbeat" to the second.)

6. "Dona nobis pacem"

Objective: Open, forte sound; syncopated beginning; entrances at high pitch levels (S, T).

a. Clap hands for the first beat of the measure. Extend the palms for the half note value and retract them for the last quarter note. Image: rocking chair, call 'o' 'ah', the mouth formation of 'o' will round the 'ah' sound. (Measures 1-7, 26-31, etc.):

b. The same with a spoken call:

c. Then sing the call:

d. Sing the theme in the alto part. Continue the rocking chair motion:

e. Complete the theme. Rocking chair motion (first as an exercise and then as an image). Use the circular mouth position for both "no*bis*" and "pa*cem*":

f. Prepare the high entrances by beginning in a comfortable range and transposing chromatically upwards. Open the body by breathing through the 'o' [o] vowel formation. (Vowel-breathing):

g. Speak the 'd' quickly and drop the jaw for the width of the vowel. Expand the 'o' mouth opening for singing in high tessitura:

h. One reaches f$^\sharp$ (and higher ranges), the syllable 'o' should be sung through the mouth formation created for the vowel 'a' [a]:

118

i. *Mass*, **Igor Stravinsky**

1. "Kyrie"

Objective: Bright, neutral, impersonal, vibrato-less sound; recitative-like, determined by rhythm.

a. Speak French nasal sounds with diaphragm pushes. A smirk on the upper lips (as if someone were uttering a slanderous phrase) will keep the tone centered. (See BI, j, aa-jj.)

tien tien ti ti ti ti   ti tien ti tien
[iɛ̃]   [i]

b. Sing the rhythms which were recited in 1,a above, assigning a bright tone syllable to each beat. Repeat immediately with text several times. Rapid alternation between martellato and staccato. (See BII, e, 27, bb and cc.):

c. Sopranos and tenors/altos and basses sing in canon. The syllables are controlled from the diaphragm and are separated from one another:

d. Sing the canon at the interval of a major second:

2. **"Gloria"**

Objective: Emphasis for tonal repetition (♪); martellato
a. Speak the consonants with firm diaphragm pressures:

sh sh sh (etc.)

b. Execute the same pattern with spoken vowel sounds. Strive for a stream of recitation. Begin with the bright, slender vowel i [i], using it as a point of reference for the placement of the other vowel formants (#18):

c. Sing the vowel in martellato style. (The syllables should not be divided from one another):

d. Sing the text in martellato style:

3. "Credo"

Objective: Tonal repetition of a recitation with and without dynamic variations (crescendo, subito piano and forte). (See #35, 38, 39, 40).

a. Open wide the breath musculature and the vocal tract during the eighth note rest. Sing the notes steadily, playfully without crescendo:

de de de (etc.)
[e]
ba ba ba   "
[a]
te te te te
pa pa pa pa

Articulate the consonants at the front of the mouth, without diaphragmatic impulses. Use the diaphragm for the sudden forte quarter notes. Clap: ♪ with flat palms, ♩ with hollow palms; or ♪ -clap hands, ♩ - stomp feet (#39):

b. Sing the same pattern on one tone with tone syllables and then with the text:

ba ba ba (etc.)
[a]
Con-fi-te - or u - num bap-tis - ma in re - mis-si - o -nem pec - ca - to - rem
[ɔ] [i][ɛ] [ɔ][u] [u][a][i] [a][i] [ɛ] [i][i] [ɔ][ɛ] [ɛ] [a] [ɔ]. [ɛ]
pa pa pa pa

c. Apply the rhythms and texts to nos. 38 and 40.

d. Transfer the preparatory phases of 38, 39 and 40 to the respective voice parts (soprano, alto, tenor, bass). Build polytonal intervals, triads and chords: SA, SAB, ST, SAT, SATB.

For #35 begin as in i,3a,b above. Practice the intervallic series of whole and half steps in each voice part at a slow tempo without crescendo. Combine the polytonal chords as above (i, 3,d). Crescendo from #35. (See h 4, a).

e. All the singers perform the soprano part for "et iterum" segment at #35 as an exercise without diaphragmatic activation. For the last three syllables, add the diaphragm impulses in martellato style.

4. "Sanctus"

Objective: Hard, forte interjections, slender piano lines.

a. In preparation for the call of "Sanctus" speak two energetic bursts of "ss" with sharp diaphragm pushes:

ss ss_____   ss ss_____   ss ss_____

b. Omit the consonants in the middle of the word "sanctus" (nc) so that the vowel sound of the word can be strengthened:

c. Sing the sharp 'double s' with hard diaphragm pushes. ('Double s' requires increased agility for consonant articulation.) Pronounce as above:

d. Add the consonants quickly. The 'n' is sustained and the 'k' is sharp:

e. The diaphragm plays an important role in the "Hosanna" section, beginning at #48, 52. Juxtaposed to this segment, the "Benedictus" requires a breath foundation for a firm support function (#50). The singers should be conscious of the difference between speech-oriented sections and cantabile passages. To demonstrate shifts from one singing style to another, create exercises which incorporate both techniques. Example: The first two measures flow easily. They should be sung with sustained bright vowels. After a catch breath, sing measures of rapid note values using buoyant diaphragm pushes. Select tone syllables which reflect the vowels of the text:

f. The same with the text:

5. "Agnus Dei"

Objective: Thick legato; no fluctuation of dynamic; minimum vibrato.

a. Foster passive breath control with consistent streams of exhaled air: f, s. Encourage the sensation of the air "streaming out" of the body with long, spoken vowels from the text:

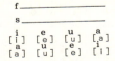

b. Sing with "gliding" breath; do not engage diaphragm activity:

c. Combine the previous exercise with a tonal pattern from the vocal score #56. Place the 'i' in front of the 'a' to give the right placement and brightness to the vowels. Hold the voice still with no dynamic changes:

d. Add the text. Think 'i' [ɪ] at the beginning. Throughout the exercise, imagine the first vowel sounding even while the second vowel is being sung:

e. Articulate all the consonants quickly from the front of the mouth, creating a "chain of vowels." Use the sustained 'm' and 'n' to insure forward placement resonance and fluency of sound:

j. *Ein deutsches Requiem*, **Johannes Brahms**

1. **"Selig sind die da Leid tragen"** (Movement #1)

Objective: Dynamic from pianissimo to forte; crescendo-decrescendo in short time spans on one tone; round, dark, warm sound; expressive use of consonants; high and low registers.

a. Prepare for soft singing and a high, forward placement with 'l'. (See B I,j,3.) (Fishmouth):

b. Develop the 'e' [e] from the darker vowels; 'e' must not sound flaccid or strident (measures 15, 19, 31). Begin with a rounded lip position for a heady sound without crescendo (rabbit teeth):

c. Transfer the 'e' [e] sound (achieved above) to the text "Selig sind". In order to match the vowel colors, think the 'i' [i] vowel for "Selig" while singing the word "sind", both vowels should be sung in the same position:

d. Practice frequent recurrences of crescendo and decrescendo with short note values (measures 40-42). The effect should be an uninterrupted, gradual increase and decrease of sound. (See B II,e,10):

e. See the same quarter-note motion during dynamic changes over longer note values. The mouth opens and closes respectively with the augmentation and diminution of the sound. (See B II,d,7 and 8.):

dö dö dö (etc.)
[ø]

f. Apply to the text. In every case, the prefixes and suffixes containing the vowel 'e' [ə] require special attention. Use the small rounded mouth opening associated with the umlaut 'ö' [œ], 'ö' [ø]. For uncomfortably high tessitura, modify the vowel to 'a' [a]:

sie sol - len ge - tröš - tet wer - den
[zi] [zo] [ə] [ə] [ø] [ə] [ve] [ə]

g. The game which was played with the mouth opening (in "e" above) is helpful for crescendo-decrescendo on one pitch as well (measures 29, 31, 61, etc.). Stretch the mouth opening over two beats and close it gradually over two beats. Lean into the sound:

nö_____ no
[ø]   [o]
ne_____ ne

h. Divide the time in half. (Think of eighth note values):

se - lig
[ze] [iç]

i. Special instruction for Sopranos: Begin in the middle range, advance by half steps upward increasing mouth space with each chromatic transposition. Sing the exercise on 'a' [a] to insure maximum resonating area in the high voice:

Sop: simile

se - lig (etc.)
[ze] [iç]

(a - opening)

j. Often when the voice part is marked "espressivo," the implication is the expressive use of the consonants to paint the text. It is a similar assignment for the solo singer as for a vocal ensemble (see foreword). In a choral context, proper coordination of the articulators and the diaphragm provides a method of group interpretation for a designated text. For example, the consonants 'tr' will be accented with a diaphragm push. The air is constricted briefly before the vowel sound is phonated. This short lapse adds a certain definition to the word "Tragen," "getroestet," "Traenen." The same principle applies to "Freude":

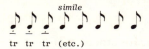

tr tr tr (etc.)

k. The expressive element is intensified when sung:

l. A similar effect can be achieved with the sustained consonants (such as 'l' [l], 'v' [v]) by anticipating the articulation of the initial consonant. (See B II,c,19.)

Maintain the coordination of articulation to diaphragm:

126

sie gehn und wei - nen
[i] [e] [u] [vəə] [ə]

espress.

sung: sie gehn und w - a - enen
[i] [e] [u][v][a] [ə ə]

2. "Denn alles Fleisch es ist wie Gras" (Movement #2)

Objective: Juxtaposition of marcato and dolce as well as forte and piano singing.

a. The composer indicates "sempre legato, ma un poco marcato" ("always sustained, but a little marked"). In order to fulfill the first requirement, the singer must not neglect the tension for notes of longer duration. Divide the half-note values into equal quarter note figures (measures 22 ff.). Sing the passage 'forte' with a diaphragm push for every note. (This exercise serves as preparation for marcato singing also.) Stretch each vowel sound. Repeat 'piano' with the same intensity as the 'forte' version:

da da da da (etc.)
[a]

b. Return to the original note value, but think the quarter note pulsation so that the longer notes do not lose energy. Sing the segment 'forte', repeat 'piano':

da da da (etc.)
[a]

c. The orchestra establishes the marcato character of this opening section. The vocal part must imitate and support the orchestral interpretation. Martellato technique (as above) and considerable exploitation of significant consonants are the tools of the choir. The singers will recognize their role if the text is spoken softly with rests inserted between the words, as if one were enunciating the phrase to a deaf person. (See B II, c 25 ee):

Denn ' alles ' Fleisch ' es ' ist ' wie ' Gras ', und ' alle '
Herrlichkeit ' des ' Menschen ' wie ' des ' Grases ' Blumen.

d. Sing the text loudly in its rhythmic context with emphasis on the consonants and weight on every vowel. Repeat softly:

e. Sing the theme with the text and with the dynamic specifications of the vocal score (measures 54-65). 'Forte' intensity during the diminuendo to 'piano':

f. Execute the dolce sections (measures 33 ff, 65 ff) on 'lü' [lʏ]. Then add the text.

g. The shape of the theme for "die Erloeseten des Herrn" which appears first in the bass (measures 20 b ff), makes it susceptible to forward motion. The eighth notes if sung too sharply will cause the passage to rush. To establish a steady pulse, divide into eighth notes all the quarter and half note values. Accompany each pitch with a gentle drop of the jaw:

h. Sing the theme in its rhythmic context. Tap the eighth-note pulsations throughout:

128

i. Maintain the image of the eighth note pulsations, so that the second half of each beat will be executed precisely in tempo. Relaxation on each quarter-note:

die Er - lö - se-ten des Herrn wer-den wie - der-kom - men (etc.)
[i] [ɛ] [ø] [ə][ə] [e] [ɛ] [ve][ə] [vi] [ə][ɔ] [ə]

j. Support the staccato words "wird weg" (measures 261 ff) with diaphragm pushes, shortening each note by half its value. Spit the final consonants. Speak the words of the text in a monotone. Sing the same text on one pitch. Conclude by singing the alto part. Deal with the word "wird" as if it were an up-beat (set apart, without emphasis). "Weg" is the downbeat with its equivalent length and emphasis:

3. "Herr, lehre doch mich" (Movement #3)

Objective: Broken chords from low to high registers; rapid eighth note groups.

a. Start with broken chords from a low tonic pitch. Begin with a small mouth opening and open the mouth progressively with the ascending intervals. Close the mouth with the descending intervals. (measures 173 ff). Imagine the broken chord in contrary motion. (See B II, d 1.):

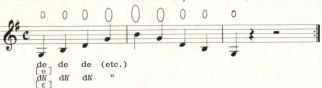

b. Transfer the falling jaw motion to the text. Remain relaxed and open. Open to 'a' [a] for the highest pitches. Prepare for this passage by vocalizing with broken chords, transposed chromatically through the key of e major. (Measure 173, also 144 ff):

der   Ge -   rech- ten See -   len
[ɐ]   [ə]   [ɛç] [ə] [ze]   [ə]
sind   in   Got- tes   Hand
[zi]   [i]   [ɔ]   [ə]   [a]

c. Sing lightly the slurred eighth note groupings: The jaw falls by its own weight. Do not allow an aspirate 'h' to occur between the notes. Define clearly the second note of each group. (measures 174,176,179, etc.):

dü   dü   (etc.)
[y]
de   de   "
[e]
dä   dä   "
[ɛ]
da   da   "
[a]

d. The same with text:

sind in Got - tes   Hand
[zi][i] [ɔ] [ə]   [a]

der   Ge - rech-ten   Seelen
[e] [ə] [ɛç] [ə]   [ze][ə]

e. Sing the entire text of the theme from the alto part. (measures 175 ff):

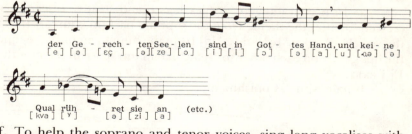

der Ge - rech - ten See-len   sind in   Got -   tes Hand, und kei- ne
[e] [ə] [ɛç]   [ə][ze] [ɔ]   [i][i]   [ɔ]   [ə] [a] [u] [ɑə] [ə]

Qual rüh -   ret sie   an   (etc.)
[kva] [Y]   [ə] [zi] [a]

f. To help the soprano and tenor voices, sing long vocalises with tone syllables. (Relaxed jaw). Add diaphragm pushes where the tempo allows. (Measures 185 ff, 202 ff.):

simile

do do do (etc.)
[o]
da da da   "
[a]

g. In the case of tonal repetitions, bind the notes together. The singer must think a new vowel for each pitch, insuring equal length and intensity of the vowels and rhythmic shapes:

ba ba ba ba (a) (etc.)
[a]

h. Sing the vocalise on 'a' [a] (Qual). Small jaw movements, diaphragm impulses when possible:

Qual_____(a)   (a)   (a)
[kva]
_____(a)

Sing the complete phrase from the vocal score (measure 185 ff, also 202 ff). Begin with the phrase from b and transpose chromatically for each repetition through e″[e′].

4. "Wie lieblich sind deine Wohnungen" (Movement #4)

Objective: legato-espressivo, bright, rounded vowels; martellato; crescendo-decrescendo.

a. In preparation for a thick legato and steady crescendo and decrescendo, hum the theme from the soprano part (measures 4 ff). Develop the vowels 'u' [u], 'o' [o], and 'a' [a] from the hum to amplify the tones. Rest the lips gently on each other to create maximum space in the mouth. (See B I,j,1,aa).

Inhale with "astonishment":

b. Sing the same passage on 'ue' [y]. Use this rounded shape (fishmouth) for the vowels 'e' [e] and 'i' [i]. Open the mouth for the crescendo and close it for the decrescendo:

c. Sing the vowels as they appear in the text. Pay attention to the vowel coloration. A rounded mouth position will neutralize strident sounds. Next, sing the text:

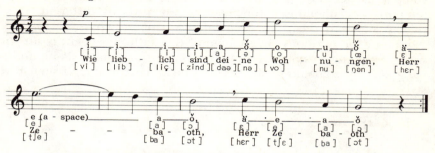

d. The expressive meaning of the words "verlanget und sehnet" ("Longing and yearning") can be augmented by the consonants. (See C II,j,2,j). Sing the 'e' [e] of "sehnet" through the hard palate. Stress the first syllable of the word; do not forget to treat the interval and final consonants carefully:

e. Use decisive diaphragm impulses to point up the "glorifying" character of the eighth note groupings (Measures 124 ff); all the notes receive the same weight. Declaim the passage as if it were an announcement. (Calling sensation):

f. Sing with the same bouncy impulses from the diaphragm:

5. "Ihr habt nun Traurigkeit", "Denn wir haben hie keine bleibende Statt" (Movements #5 and #6)

Objective: Cultivation of contrasting vocal techniques: legato (cantabile); mezza voce (half voice), and portato (piano).

a. Movements #5 and #6 have the same dynamic markings (piano) comparable tempo indications [langsam (slow); tempo/andante (moving tempo)]. The diaphragm functions in two distinctly different ways for these passages. In the fifth movement, the diaphragm passively sustains the motion of the harmony. Every note of the sixth movement is supported with a light and flexible diaphragm pressure (martellato). Point out these variations by combining phrases of similar length and dissimilar vocal styles:

b. To achieve the brilliance and warmth which denotes the word "troesten" (to comfort), modify the 'oe' [ø] vowel to 'ue' [Y] in the upper register. (Movement #5, measure 20, 22, etc.):

c. The opening pitches of the sixth movement (measures 3 ff) require substantial weight despite the piano dynamic. Ask the singers to tiptoe over each note in 4/4 time. Whisper the theme in rhythm, imitating the profound character of the text:

d. Continue stepping to the music while singing the phrase softly (Note the diaphragm impulses):

Denn wir ha - ben hier kei - - - ne blei - ben - de Statt.
[ɛ] [vi] [a] [ə] [i] [a] [ɔ][ə] [a] [ə][ə] [ə] [a]

e. The inhalation for the vivace (Movement #6, measures 82 ff) should occur with a 'forte' feeling. Each singer speaks the rhythm of each respective voice part (measures 82 ff, 99 ff) 'forte', treating each note as if it were marked 'staccato' (short, sharp accentuated with stout diaphragmatic impulses). Sing the text on one note and then to the pitches of the musical context:

Denn es wird die Po - sau - ne schal -
[ɛ] [ɛ] [vi] [i] [o] [za] [ɔ][ə] [ʃ][a]

- - len. und wir wer - den ver -
[ə] [u] [vi] [ve] [ə] [fɛ]

wan - delt, ver - wan - delt wer - den.
[va] [ə] [fɛ] [va] [ə] [ve] [ə]

6. "Selig sind die Toten" (Movement #7)

Objective: Depth and roundness of the forte sound.

a. Develop the 'piano' "selig" using the consonant 'l' as described for the equivalent passage in the first movement. (See B I, j 3). The "selig" marked 'forte' should be negotiated with deep breath support and body awareness for proper phonation and vowel coloration. Inhale as if "astonished" and call out in "wonderment:" 'ah'. Begin the vowel very high and carry the sound through the range of the voice (squaling). (See B I,k,5). Do the same activity with the vowels 'o' [o], 'e' [e].

b. Sigh and sing the same vowels with the same open body sensation:

c. Choose the texts which evoke astonishment: Sing with the sensation of calling. Begin with a wide space:

Oh,			how beau- ti -	ful	the	sun -		shine!
Hal	-	-	le - -	lu -	ja,	a -		men!
Glo	-	-	ri -	a,	ho -	san -		na!

d. The sopranos and tenors sing the entire passage in their range. (measures 2 ff, 103 ff). Encourage openness for the attack by beginning the exercise on 'a' [a] and gradually gliding the tongue to 'e' [e] retaining the rounded mouth/lips position of 'ah' [a] for the 'e' [e] vowel:

e. Attack the 'e' [e], but cling to the image of 'a' [a]. This principle holds for the 'e' vowel in the word "sterben" (to die) as well:

GLOSSARY

ACCENT: From the Latin word *accentus* meaning "emphasis," implies *sforzato*. 1. Strong diaphragmatic impulse under a consonant and its accompanying vowel, resulting in a slight decrescendo. 2. A gentle preparation for a tone.

ARTICULATION: 1. Verbal: the flexibility of jaw, lips, tongue and soft palate independent of the vowel sounds which are phonated in their chamber (the vocal tract). These processes are connected by the coordination of diaphragmatic activity to create clear pronunciation of text. 2. Musical: the manner of separating or combining two or more tones. Such practices are indicated in musical notation by phrase markings, staccato points, etc. An important element of interpretation.

BOURDON: From the French word meaning "drone bass."
An interval or chord (octave, fifth, triad) which is sustained by the lowest voices (bagpipe).

BREATHINESS: Excess air which is not gathered into the phonated tone veils the vocal sound. Young women exhibit this vocal problem often (during puberty). When it occurs in older singers, its cause may be inadequate breath support, overt muscular support or extensive force upon the voice.

BREATH INTERVAL: After allowing the breath to fall into the body, take a few seconds (breath interval) to imagine the sound of the tone, its pitch, dynamic and character before proceeding to sing.

CANTABILE: From the Latin word "cantus" meaning to sing; singable. (See Legato)

CATCH BREATH: Sudden intake of air by widening the breath mechanism, allowing the atmospheric air to "fall into" the body. (Imagine a passive "snap" for breath.)

CHEST QUALITY: A sound which evolves from exploiting the chest voice during the modulation to notes of the middle range.

CLOSURE OF THE VOCAL CORDS (FOLDS): Flexibility of the vocal lips, which approximate (draw together). The character of the sound of the voice depends upon the capability of the singer to produce a complete closure of the vocal cords.

CLUSTER: A bundle of tones which stand together without harmonic structure or relation.

COLORATURA: From the Latin word "colorare" meaning to color; in singing, the term implies the coloration or ornamentation of the vocal line. A virtuoso flourish or running passage in solo or ensemble repertoire; especially defined in Baroque music, more flexible in the music of the Classic era.

CONSISTENCY OF REGISTERS: Through the help of resonance, vowel modification and even gradations of tonal volume, the three registers of the human voice (see Registers) should melt into one consistent series of sounds. The chest register will not be exploited into the middle register nor the head voice carried into the lower voice.

COVERED SOUND: See also "head quality." A sound which is placed in the back of the head. Such a tone will exhibit roundness and aural transparency.

DEEP BREATHING: A type of breathing for singers which uses the strength of the muscles in the lower rib cage, sides and back to support the movement of the diaphragm. The upper part of the body where the voice box resides remains passive and relaxed. It is important to establish a feeling of openness (astonishment). See also "intercostal breathing."

DIAPHRAGM: A muscular plate drawn through the body dividing the chest cavity with lungs and heart from the abdominal area. When the diaphragm is at rest (after exhalation) it forms a dome under the ribcage. During inhalation the diaphragm lowers, forming a floor for the expanded lungs, adjusting the internal organs downwards. The diaphragm is the most important muscle in the singer's breath mechanism.

DIPHTHONG: Double vowel. In the English language: ay [ei̯], o [ou̯], ow [au̯] ie [ai̯], oi [ɔi̯].

DYNAMICS: Variations in tonal volume (forte, piano, etc.)

FALSETTO: From the Latin word "falsus" meaning false. A fourth register in the male voice (beside chest, middle and head). It sounds when the whistle voice is intensified through chest resonance. The falsetto range extends far above the natural high voice and manifests a distinct color and quality difference.

FISHMOUTH: Formation of the lips in a rounded position to give the tone direction and uniform shape. This formation will serve also to open the vocal tract.

FLACCID SINGING: Flaccid singing results from phonation without resonance and body connection (width).

FUNCTION OF THE FRINGE: Vibration of the fringes of the vocal folds, providing an amplification of head resonance in the sound.

GLISSANDO: From the French term "glisser" meaning to glide. A manner of performance involving a slide of the voice between pitches without definite intervallic gradations.

GLOTTAL ATTACK: Forced attack; the approximation of the vocal cords will be forced by the sudden phonation of a vowel. Such a method of phonation will produce improper closure of the vocal cords, if used in excess (a habit prevalent among untrained singers). The method should be used sparingly. It is an expressive technique in the music of the avant-garde. It can be therapeutic for complete closure of the vocal folds under professional guidance.

HEAD QUALITY: The sound indicative of the head voice (head resonance, not head register), piano.

HIGH VOCAL PLACEMENT: Also called "forward placement"; the point of focus for the vocal tone. Frontal area of the palate, teeth, "between the eyes."

INTERCOSTAL BREATHING: Important body function which adds support to the lower ribcage for more efficient breath control (back and sides). The intercostal muscles work together to hold the diaphragm in its optimal position for the support of a singing tone.

INTONATION: Accuracy of tonality (high, low). Sources of poor intonation: among others, poor breath control, fatigue, hearing deficiency relating to harmonic context of musical passage, vocal/technical difficulties such as inadequate or profuse support of sound, inconsistent registration, improper vowel modification, insufficient head or chest quality.

LEGATO: From the Latin term "ligatura" meaning connection. The combining of tones without interruption of the stream of sound. For wind players: without tongue articulation; for string players: without bow attack; for singers: without new vowel attack (as a vocalise). In a textual setting: brisk and swift enunciation of consonants, long, sustained vowels.

MARTELLATO: From the Italian word for "hammer"; each tone is given a diaphragmatic impulse, so that a slight accent emerges without completely separating the sounds. The sound is "hammered." Martellato technique is used for coloratura passages and sharp rhythmic flourishes (Baroque) and for word or syllabic underscoring or accent (Baroque, Romantic, Modern).

MASK: Belongs to head voice. Resonance in the frontal region (see also covered sound). Mask resonance amplifies and directs the sound by creating a core of focus (high vocal placement).

MESSA DI VOCE: A tone which swells and diminishes. Used in Italian bel canto technique as ornamentation. Indicated by crescendo-decrescendo marks over a sustained tone.

MESSA VOCE: Half voice.

NASAL: A sound captured in the nasal region; not to be confused with nasal resonance, which is an important part of mask resonance.

OPEN THROAT: Relaxed position of vocal mechanism; a flexible "suspension" of the mechanism achieved through proper relationship of tension and relaxation in all adjoining regions.

PARLANDO: From the French word "parler" to speak; a syllabic tonal setting whereby each tone is spoken or sung with quick, energetic and flexible articulation.

PHRASING: Significant relation of musical and textual elements in a melodic context (thematic groupings, structural shaping).

PLACEMENT: Tonal attack through intuitive imagination. The singer recalls the position, pitch, dynamic, color and character of the sound before phonation.

PORTATO: From the Latin term "portare" to carry; an art of singing between legato and martellato. The singer carries the sound from tone to tone; each tone will be confronted with a new vowel sound to give it character and equality (without diaphragmatic impulse).

REGISTER: The muscles of the vocal mechanism do not work simultaneously without the balance between breath pressure, vowel formation and vibrations of the vocal folds. If some element fails to function, the sound of the voice will deteriorate. One associates this failure with a particular region of the voice (head, middle, chest). In an ideal case (a natural voice, a well-trained singer) one recognizes only one register to sound without distinct "levels."

RESONANCE: From the Latin word "resonare" to resound; the sound which is phonated in the throat by the vibration of the vocal folds is not audible acoustically without amplification. The sound is directed to the bony regions of the body and face where it meets with a resistance which increases and develops the sound.

SFORZATO: See Accent.

STACCATO: Very short tones directed from the diaphragm.

SUPPORT: Also called "breath management"; the lungs (chest cavity) expand as a tone is sung as do the diaphragm, the abdominal wall, the sides and back. The singer who approximates the vocal cords completely, will suspend the air between these "poles," providing support to the tone. The poles represent a floor to the sound and a high point of focus.

THROAT AREA: The moveable chamber in which the vocalis muscle resides, surrounded by the thyroid, the arytenoid and the cricoid cartilages, positioned at the top of the wind pipe, extending to the pharynx.

TONE SYLLABLE: A consonant and vowel combination, used for the instruction of a segment of a choral work. The syllable is chosen for its vocal technical application, and as a preservation of vocal and textual resources.

TREMOLO: Exaggerated vibrato such that the voice shivers. A voice plagued by a tremolo is out of control and of little use. Possible causes: inadequate breath support, tension in the jaw and/or vocal tract, nervousness.

VIBRATO: Vibration of a freely phonated voice. Vibrato determines the activity, sentiment and beauty of the sound.

VOICE PART: The characteristic sound and range of the voice is considered in selecting which voice part a chorister should sing. General distribution: (different from singer to singer): Bass, e to F, Baritone G-g, Tenor

C-a', Alto F-f2, Soprano c-b2. As voices are trained, the ranges will expand or adjust.

VOICED FRICATIVE CONSONANTS: Use of friction between lips, tongue and/or teeth to produce a consonant sound (examples, l, v, dj, z: [l] [v] [dʒ] [z]).

VOICED NASAL CONSONANTS: The sustainable consonant sounds m, n, ng [m] [n] [ŋ]) which resonate in the nasal passages.

VOCAL TRACT: The vocal mechanism which produces and amplifies sound. Parts of the tract include the laryngeal region (voice box, vocalis muscle, vocal cords/lips/folds), the pharyngeal region and its adjacent pathways, the mouth area and the resonating cavities.

VOWELS (open/closed): Closed vowels: a [a] mat, a [e] may, e [i] me, o [o] so, u [u] moon. Open vowels: a [a] father, e [ɛ] met, I [ɪ] mit, o [ɔ] paw, u [ʊ] foot. The term "open" vowel has a double meaning in its particular application to singing. When a word begins with an "open" vowel, the word may need to be set apart from other vowels or consonants to maintain its clarity. Elision can confuse the words and thus the listener:

*A*nd *A*lice *a*nswered *a*lso (open vowels).

Through elision, an "open" vowel may be considered closed.

VOWEL BREATHING: A sensation for the succeeding vowel. One feels in the mouth, lips, tongue, vocal tract, resonating area the sensation of the vowel which is to be sung. This sensitivity is creating during inhalation. The vowel is heard as the air is consumed. The more intense the imagination, the more precise and secure the vowel and tone.

VOWEL MODIFICATION: Mixture of bright vowels (i [i], e [e], a [a]) with dark vowels (u [u] o [o]) to acquire a consistency in the registers of the voice, improve intonation or create a specific tonal character.

MUSIC EXAMPLES

BIBLIOGRAPHY

Egenolf, Heinrich. *Die Menschliche Stimme.* Stuttgart: Paracelsus Verlag
GMBH, 1974

Gümmer, Paul. *Erziehung der Menschlichen Stimme.* Kassel: Bärenreiter
Verlag. 1962

Hofbauer, Kurt. *Praxis der Chorischen Stimmbildung.* Mainz: Schott Verlag,
1978

Iro, Otto. *Diagnostik und Paedagogik der Stimmbildung.* Wiesbaden: Rudolf
Erdmann Verlag, 1961

Kemper, Josef. *Stimmpflege.* Mainz: Schott Verlag, 1951

Lohmann, Paul. *Stimmfehler, Stimmberatung.* Mainz: Schott Verlag, 1966

Martienssen-Lohmann, Franziska. *Ausbildung der Gesangs-Stimme.* Wiesbaden: Rudolf Erdmann Verlag, 1957

Martienssen-Lohmann, Franziska. *Der Wissende Saenger.* Zuerich: Atlantis
Verlag, 1956

Nitsche, Paul. *Die Pflege der Kinder- und Jugendstimme.* Mainz: Schott Verlag,
1969

Riesch, Anneliese. *Lebendige Stimme.* Mainz: Schott Verlag, 1972

Thomas, Franz. *Belcanto.* Berlin: Georg Achterberg Verlag, 1968

Witte, Gerd. *Grundriss Einer Chorischen Stimmbildung.* Kassel: Bärenreiter
Verlag, 1963